NOTICE OF TERMS OF USE

I0479240

i

FORWARD

This book fills a gap that has existed for too long now and has been written by and insurance valuation practitioner as a practical guide for computing the sums insured or value at risk for various properties. The book enables the reader to understand the fundamental principles of valuation and relate them to the various insurance aspects to arrive at the right sums insured. It provides more approaches to the reader on the various methods of valuing properties. It provides a number of practical examples that the enhance the readers understanding of the concept.

Farid Ssenfuka

TABLE OF CONTENTS

iv

1.0 INTRODUCTION

Many insurance companies and loss adjusters face challenges in computing the sums insured or value at risks for various properties. Some of them instead use bank valuation reports for insurance purposes. It is important to note that bank valuation reports are purposely intended for banking purposes and these guide the bank on market and forced sale values of properties or securities belonging to loan applicants. Majority of the insurance values recommended in these reports tend to have a wrong basis since most valuers lack a clear understanding of the various insurance principles of reinstatement and or indemnity. In most cases, the market, forced sale and insurance values in these reports are land inclusive and provide inaccurate or misguiding values.

Insurance asset valuations operate on a totally different principle and are usually based on the cost of replacing the asset in case its damaged. When a claim is made, it draws funds from the pool of insurance premiums paid by all policyholders. Some under declared property values may cost more to repair or replace. [1, 2] Majority policyholders under declare their assets while trying to avoid higher premiums. Some simply provide a single block figure for all their property which makes it difficult to establish whether a given item was adequately Insured or not.

Another key attribute of insurance asset valuation arises when calculating the value at risk (VAR) in insurance claims which depicts whether an item was under insured, over Insured or adequately Insured. Many loss adjusters cannot independently comment on the value at risk and most of them have to rely on the policyholder's documents and may not be in position to advise the Insurer whether the sums insured are adequate thus making the Insurer pay large sums of cash in situations where the average clause would otherwise apply. Establishing the right VAR not only helps during claim adjustments but also helps in making the relevant policy adjustments and increased premiums for the previously under declared assets.

Many Loss adjusters often fail to effectively comment on the precise salvage value of the affected asset or its components and neither can they advise on the scrap value of the asset and potential markets or buyers to enable the insurer make some minimum recoveries following an admitted loss.

This book provides a number of approaches to guide the reader in attaining the right property values or sums Insured for purposes of attaining the right premiums. It also provides a guide for computing the value at risk and salvage valuation during Loss adjustment.

1.1 The term "valuation"

The term valuation can be defined as a professional judgement of the worthiness of something. It is sometimes defined as an estimation of the worthiness of something or an asset. In finance, its often defined as the process of determining the present value of an asset. Generally, valuation is both a science and an art. It includes components and knowledge of mathematics, statistics, sociology and common sense among other factors.

1.2 Purpose of valuations

- Insurance
- Bank valuations
- Purchasing for Investment
- Purchasing for self-Occupation
- Mergers and acquisitions
- Rent Fixation
- Arbitration
- Taxation
- Disposal
- Mortgaging

1.3 Importance of insurance valuations

- Providing a starting point for an accurate sum Insured.
- Providing a breakdown of the sum Insured for the block figures submitted by the policy holder.
- Reassurance that the sum Insured on the policy schedule is as accurate as possible such that, in the event of a total loss, sufficient funds are available to settle the claim.
- Providing an accurate estimate of the reinstatement costs especially for buildings, bridges, dams & drainages channels, fences among other structures.
- Providing an accurate estimate of the replacement and or repair costs for the personal property, household items, office equipment, machinery, vehicles including the freight charges etc.

1.4 Essentials of a good valuation

- Proper understanding of valuation instructions.
- Proper selection of the most appropriate valuation method.
- Practical or technical knowledge of the valuation assignment.
- Proper selection and use of valuation tools or equipment.
- Thorough field data collection
- Good communications skills.
- Thorough analysis of availed information and documents.
- Good report writing skills and use of acceptable report formats.

1.5 Sources of valuation data

- <u>Physical inspections:</u> Physical inspections are key in property valuations as they confirm the presence of the asset and its condition at the time of inspection. These protect the Insurer from issuing policies against faulty and damaged property in order to get rid of any potential fraudulent claims. During these inspections, the machine operators may be required to start or run the machines and operate it in the presence of the valuer who may be in position to tell if it is in a good working condition.

- <u>Interaction with staff:</u> Due the limited survey time and report deadlines, the valuer may need to use more tactics in acquiring the relevant information about the property. This includes interactions with the asset users or operators to understand the asset specification and working condition which may include its function, model, year of installation or commissioning, working condition, defects and faults in the machine.

- <u>Property use and maintenance:</u> The valuer is usually required to attain information relating to the asset function work, frequency of use, working environment, operator skill among other factors. They client is also required to present or submit maintenance or service reports for the property or equipment to show the frequency of maintenance. They should provide details of the types maintenance that is done which include periodic, preventive and or conditional maintenance. All this information may guide the valuer in attaining a suitable asset depreciation rate.

- <u>Internet:</u> Of late, e-commerce has evolved worldwide and companies are able to market their products around the globe using the internet. As such, the valuer can attain multiple equipment valuations/prices from various suppliers in the world. Internet also presents local and regional marketing platforms that allow trade amongst multiple buyers and sellers. These sources also provide a good basis for attaining a market value of the asset as explained in the proceeding sections.

1.6 Data collection tools

There are a number of tools that can be used in gathering information and drafting a good valuation report and these may include the following;

- Checklist: A valuer can make use of a check list to note the various aspects of property valuation. For example, a vehicle valuation checklist could look out for the condition of the engine, suspension system, braking system, electrical system, tyres, defects on the body, panels, windscreen, previous ownership, year of purchase and purchase amount among others.

- Interview guide: The surveyor can make use of the interview guide to gather data relating the property, its users, frequency of use, nature of use, age and or maintenance rate among other facts that can assist in the valuation process.

- Questionnaires: Alternatively, the valuer can issue a questionnaire to the client to fill at their most convenient time. These questionnaires are usually designed to gather information that may not have been provided during the physical inspection or survey.

- Note book: A surveyor's note book is the most important data collection tool which contributes to a good survey report. It basically records the all information gathered during the survey that would assist the valuer in drafting a valuation report. Visiting the fields without a notebook puts the valuer in trouble since they cannot memorize all the aspects pertaining to the valuation assignment.

- Digital cameras: Photographic evidence is very important in supporting the survey report. It serves as proof of the exact property and condition. Since photographs speak volumes, the surveyor should take photos of all the relevant aspects which they would wish to elaborate in their report.

- Tape measure: During the survey, a valuer may be required to note the details of certain equipment or structures including asset, buildings and or machinery dimensions. By using the tape measure, they are able to record the building plinth area, boundary wall length, width and thickness which may aid in attaining their replacement or depreciated values.

2.0 MAJOR VALUATION PRINCIPLES & TERMS

2.1 Fundamental principles of valuation

1. Cost – It is the expenditure to produce a commodity having a value. It also means the original cost of an item i.e. vehicle, furniture, machinery etc. In the construction industry cost means the original cost of the construction including the cost of materials and labour. <u>Hence the cost is a</u> **FACT.**

2. Price – It is the cost of a commodity or construction plus additional reward (profit margin) to the producer for his labour and capital. The profit or additional reward may be varied from one producer to another depending on the existing market forces of demand and supply among other factors. <u>Hence price is a</u> **POLICY.**

3. Value – Valuation is an opinion or an estimate which will be determined by many factors like the purpose, supply, demand, depreciation, obsolescence etc. Valuation is a function of place, date and purpose. <u>Hence value is an</u> **OPINION.**

2.2 Major valuation terms

a. Market Value – Is defined by the International Valuation Standards (IVS 2022) as the estimated amount for which an asset or liability should exchange hands on the date of valuation between a willing buyer and willing seller in an arms length's transaction after proper marketing wherein the parties had each acted knowledgeably, prudently and without compulsion.

It is simply the price that is currently offered for the asset at the market place. It can also be defined as the value of the property if it is sold in the open market. It can be attained or established after depreciating the replacement value. Its sometimes defined as the Actual Cash Value with literally means the amount equal to the replacement cost minus depreciation of a damaged property at the time of the loss or valuation. It can also be established by obtaining recent quotations from various suppliers, dealers or contractors among other service providers.

b. Forced Sale Value: By International Valuation Standards (IVS 2022) refers to circumstances where a seller is under compulsion to sell and that as a consequence, a proper marketing period is not possible and buyers may not be able to undertake adequate due diligence.

c. Depreciation – Depreciation is the gradual exhaustion of the usefulness of a property. This may be defined as the gradual decrease in the value of an asset over time. Usually a percentage on depreciation per annum is considered. The depreciation rate can be based on the following factors;

- Original cost
- Physical appearance
- Structural properties
- Useful life span
- Period in use
- Rate of use
- Environment of use
- Product specifications & technology rating
- Rate of maintenance
- Wear & tear
- Obsolescence
- Scrap value or salvage value

d. Replacement / Reinstatement Value – This can be generally defined as the cost of replacing an old asset with a new one. In an Insurance context especially claims, it is the cost of replacing or reinstating the damaged item/ property with the same kind or type but not superior to or more extensive than the insured property when new. It also represents the cost of re-constructing the entire structure/building in case of a total loss or partial damage. The new item should not be significantly better in terms of specifications like size, capacity, technology, manufacturer, year of manufacture among others. In some insurance policies the replacement cost includes other items like freight and installation among other incidental costs.

e. Life span and useful life – The asset life span is usually longer than its useful life. For example, a machine can have a life span of 30years with a useful life of 15 years depending on a number of factors including its usage rate and maintenance. The asset useful life concerns the amount of time an asset is expected to be fully functional and perform according the user expectations or standards. It also known as economic life or service life. The useful life normally ends when the asset performance drastically declines and it is unable to operate normally as required. The asset life span is usually longer than its useful life.

f. Book Value – This is an accounting term used to measure a business's equity and value of assets that appear on the balance sheet. Most accountants arrive at the asset book value by depreciating its initial cost. The depreciation usually considers its period of use.

c. Residual value – Is the value of the asset after exhausting its useful lifespan. This is the remaining value that an asset possesses. This greatly depends on its physical state, period in use and current working condition among other factors. It is sometimes defined us as the disposal value.

h. Salvage Value – Is the value of the asset after damage and greatly depends on the extent of damage or loss, its physical state and current working condition. If the item is severely damaged beyond repair, it can be regarded as scrap.

i. Scrap Value (Junk Value) – Is the value of a more useless item after attaining old age or excessive damage or completing its usefulness. This greatly depends on its physical state and condition of the asset.

j. Value at Risk (VAR) – Is a statistical technique used to measure and quantify the level of financial risk within a firm or investment portfolio over a specific time frame. It is normally measured in three variables i.e. the amount of potential loss, the probability of that amount of loss and time frame. The value at risk is also used to measure the maximum loss that a portfolio of assets could suffer over a given time horizon with a specific level of confidence.

In an Insurance and claim context, this can mean the value of an asset at a given time i.e. at policy inception, prior to damage or after a loss. In most cases, VAR is used to estimate the value of an asset prior to a loss i.e. when computing the adequacy of sum insured. The VAR greatly depends on the issued insurance policy and its wording. The basis of asset valuation in some policies is on replacement or reinstatement basis while others are on indemnity basis. In the former case. this means that no depreciation is considered when determining the value of the asset prior to the loss. In the latter case, depreciation is considered or applied when establishing the pre-accident value of an asset.

3.0 VALUATION METHODS

These methods are based on the asset type and or profession executing the task i.e. Accountant or Engineer. Generally, the method used should be able to provide an accurate insurance value of the asset under consideration.

3.1 Method selection criteria

Below are some of factors considered when determining the most appropriate valuation method;

- Nature of assignment
- Nature of property/asset
- Complexity of the assignment
- Availed documents or information
- Prevailing market condition i.e. supply and demand
- Total cost of reinstatement / replacement
- Time of valuation
- Assignment timeline.

3.2 Valuation professions

Below are some of the methods applied by various professions which may include and are not limited to the following;

- Business analysis: Accountants / Staticians & other business-related professions
- Structure construction: Quantity surveyors / Civil Engineers/ Structural Engineers
- Industrial plant & machinery and vehicles: Mechanical / Electrical Engineers/ Industrial Engineers

3.3 Valuation methods

Below are some valuation methods for various assets.

3.3.1 Discounted Cash Flow (DCF) method

The discounted cash flows (DCF) is one of the most detailed and justifiable ways to value a business. Under this approach, the valuer organizes the expected cash flows of the company, based on extrapolations of its historical cash flow and expectations that can be achieved. A discount rate is then applied to these cash flows to arrive at a current valuation for the business. [29] Under this method the value of an asset is computed by discounting the future cash flows attributable to the asset.

The depreciation here is defined as a measure of change in the discounted value of the asset. This means depreciation is the difference between the value of the asset based on the discounted future cash flow at the beginning of the period and the discounted future cash flow at the end of the period.

Formula

- Let's assume V = Present value of future cash flows. It is also known as DCF which defined as the is the sum of all future discounted cash flows that the investment is expected to produce.
- D = Periodic depreciation, R= Periodic cash flows (i.e. R_1, R_2, R_3, ... R_n to be the respective cash flow at the end of the period 1,2, 3,......n). It is also known as CF which is the total cash flow for a given year. $CF_1(R1)$ is for the first year, CF_2 (R_2) is for the second year, and so on. [26]
- I = Rate of interest or discount rate in decimal term. The discount rate is basically the target rate of return that you want on the investment. n = life of the assets in years.

Value of an asset at the beginning of the year:

$$V_0 = \frac{R\,1}{(1+i)} + \frac{R2}{(1+i)^{\wedge}2} + \frac{R3}{(1+i)^{\wedge}3} + \ldots\ldots + \frac{Rn}{(1+i)^{\wedge}n}$$

$$\text{Or } V_0 = \sum_{j=1}^{n} \frac{Rj}{(1+i)^{\wedge}j}$$

Then the value of the asset at the end of the first year

$$V_1 = \frac{R2}{(1+i)} + \frac{R3}{(1+i)^2} + \frac{R4}{(1+i)^3} + \ldots\ldots + \frac{Rn}{(1+i)^{n-1}}$$

$$\text{Or } V_1 = \sum_{j=2}^{n} \frac{Rj}{(1+i)^{j-1}}$$

Depreciation in year 1

$D = V_0 - V_1$

Depreciation in year 2

$D = V_1 - V_2$

Example 1:

Peter has USD 1,000 today, and compounded it at a rate of 14.5% per year, how much would he have after three years?

Solution

$DCF = CF_1 / (1+r)^n$

$1,000 = CF_1 / (1+0.145)^3$

$CF_1 = 1,000 \times 1+0.145)^3$

$= \underline{USD\ 1,501}$

3.3.2 Book Value Method

The book value literally means the value of a business according to the books of accounts. An asset's book value is equal to its value on the balance sheet, and companies calculate it by netting the asset against its accumulated depreciation. [4] Book value can also be defined as the amount that shareholders would receive if a company's assets, liabilities, and preferred stock were sold or paid off at exactly the amounts at which they are recorded in the company's accounting records. It is highly unlikely that this would actually take place, because the market value at which these items would be sold or paid off might vary by substantial amounts from their recorded values. [28]

Formula

Book value = Value on balance sheet – Accumulated depreciation

---

Example 2:

Purchase value of a machine on receipt / invoice is USD 500. Accumulated depreciation for the past 10 years is USD 100. Find the current machine value.

Solution
Book value = Value on balance sheet – Accumulated depreciation
= USD 500 – USD 100   = <u>USD 400</u>

3.3.3 Comparison method or analysis

This is the most widely used method of valuation. It uses a direct comparison with prices paid for similar properties to the one being valued. Assets to be valued must be similar in terms of specifications. The prevailing market conditions must be considered.

Example 3:

A vehicle price can be estimated after comparison with the existing models on the market especially those with similar specs as the one under consideration. Similarly, a construction rate for a building with similar construction technology can be used to compute the value of the building under consideration and putting into other factors like price of materials, location and or inflation as discussed in the sections below.

3.3.4 Depreciation method

Some of the major depreciation methods include;

a. <u>Straight line method</u> – In this method, it is assumed that the property loses its value by the same amount every year. A fixed amount of depreciation is deducted every year, so that at the end of the utility period only the scrap value is left. The present value minus salvage value is distributed uniformly for its service life.

Formula

Annual depreciation = $\dfrac{\text{Original cost} - \text{Scrap value}}{\text{Useful life span}}$

Example 4:

The purchase value of a machine on the invoice is USD 1,000. Scrap value after its useful lifespan of 15 years is USD 100. Find the machine value after 3 years.

Solution

Annual dep. = $\dfrac{\text{Original cost} - \text{Scrap value}}{\text{Useful life span}}$

$$= \dfrac{1000 - 100}{15} = \text{USD 60 per year}$$

Depreciation after 3 years = 60 x3 = USD 180

Machine value after 3 years = ([1000 – 100] – 180)

$$= \underline{USD\ 720}$$

Example 5:

The cost/ value of the building is USD 1,200,000. Considering its construction technology, the building useful life span is 60 years. Its salvage value at the end of 60 years is USD 200,000. Find the building value after 15 years.

Solution

Annual dep. = $\dfrac{\text{Original cost} - \text{Scrap value}}{\text{Useful life span}}$

$$= \dfrac{1,200,000 - 200,000}{60} = \text{USD 16,667 per year}$$

Total depreciation after 15 years = 16,667 x15 = USD 250,000

Building value after 15 years = 1,200,000 – 250,000

$$= \underline{USD\ 950,000}$$

---

b. *Declining balance method* – This is also known as the diminishing balance method or written down value method. In this method, a depreciation percentage remains constant through the life of the asset. But the capital sum or base goes on reducing every year by an amount equal to the depreciation of previous year. Thus, the quantum of depreciation in this method will go on reducing every year.

Formula

- Let's assume C = Original cost of the asset, D = Depreciable value i.e total depreciation during the service life of an asset, S= Scrap value / residual value = (C – D), n = Estimated life of asset, r = rate of depreciation in decimal term, V = book value at the end of a period, d = depreciation at the end of a period. If depreciation and the book value are reducing at a constant rate, then

$r = 1 - [(C - D)/C]^{1/n}$
$d_n = Cr [1 - r]^{n-1}$
$V_n = C [1 - r]^n$

If depreciation is not constant for each period, then; $d_t = Cr [1 - r]^{t-}$ where t = Estimated life of an asset ranging from 0 to n.

Example 6:

Building reinstatement value is JSD 4,000,000. Depreciction per year is 2%. The building age is 20 years. Find the building value.

Solution
$V_n = C [1 - r]^n$
= 4,000,000 [1 – 2/100] ^ 20
= 4,000,000 [0.98] ^ 20
= 4,000,000 [0.6676]
= USD 2,670,432

---

c. Sum of year digits – Under this method the cost less salvage value is charged to different years in the ratio of capital blocked in the asset in the year concerned to the total blockage over its life. This method assumes that depreciation of the first year should be the highest as no portion of the capital has been recovered till then and the depreciation of the last year should be the least of all years because a major portion of the invested capital has been already recovered.

Since depreciation is measured according to the volume of blocked investment, its magnitude is expressed by means of a fraction. The denominator of the fraction, which remains constant is the total of the digits representing the useful life of the asset. The numerator, on the other hand, measuring the blockage of capital in the reverse weighted digits of each year. [8]

Formula

- Let's assume D_t = Depreciation in period t, C= Cost of the asset, S = Estimated Salvage value of the asset, n = estimated life of the asset in years, t = The year of life of the asset (i.e. 1 is the first year, 2 is the second year and so on)

$$\sum_{i=1}^{n} Yi = \text{the sum of digits from 1 to n} = \frac{n(1+n)}{2}$$

The formula for measuring depreciation for a particular year is:

$$D_t = [C - S] \times \frac{n+1-t}{\sum_{i=1}^{n} Yi}$$

Example 7:

A Computer Company has purchased some computers worth USD 5,000,000. It cost them USD 200,000 to transport the Computer to their location. The Company considers that the useful life of Computers is 5 years and they can dispose the computers at a value of USD 100,000. Create a depreciation schedule for the asset using the Sum of year depreciation method.[22]

Solution	Depreciation expense for second year
Depreciable Amount	= 5,100,000 x 4/15 = 1,360,000
Total Acquisition Cost = 5,000,000 + 200,000	Book Value after second year
= 5,200,000	= 3,400,000 – 1,360,000 = 2,040,000
Salvage Value = 100,000	
Useful life of Computers = 5 years	Depreciation expense for third year
Depreciation Amount = Acqtn Cost – Salvage	= 5,100,000 x 3/15 = 1,020,000
Value	Book value after third year
= 5,200,000 – 100,000	= 2,040,000 – 1,020,000 = 1,020,000
= USD 5,100,000	
Sum of Useful Life	Depreciation expense for fourth year
Sum of useful life = 5 + 4 + 3 + 2 + 1	= 5,100,000 x 2/15 = 680,000
= 15	Book value after fourth year
Depreciation Factors for various years	= 1,020,000 – 680,000 = 340,000
Year 1 – 5/15	

Year 2 – 4/15 Year 3 – 3/15 Year 4 – 2/15 Year 5 – 1/15 Depreciation expense for first year = 5,100,000 x 5/15 = 1,700,000 Book Value after first year = 5,100,000 – 1,700,000 = 3,400,000	Depreciation expense for five year = 5,100,000 x 1/15 = 340,000 Book value after five years = 340,000 – 340,000 = USD 0 (Asset becomes obsolete)

d. *Double declining balance method* – This method may be identified as a combination of straight line and diminishing balance method. Like the diminishing balance method, the depreciation is charged on the opening written down value of the fixed asset. Like the straight-line method, a fixed rate of depreciation is charged in this method. But the rate used is twice the straight-line rate. [9]

Formula: DDB % = (100% / Lifetime) × 2

Example 8:

A company bought a machine for USD 100,000. They have estimated the useful life of the machine to be 8 years. Find its value after the 8 years. [23]

Solution

Now, as per the straight-line method of depreciation:
Cost of the asset = USD 100,000
Salvage Value = USD 11,000
The useful life of the asset = 8 years
Depreciation rate = 1/useful life *100 = (1/8) * 100 = 12.5%
Double-declining balance formula = 2 X Cost of the asset X Depreciation rate.
Here, it will be 2 x 12.5% = 25%
Year 1 Depreciation = USD100000 X 25% = USD 25,000
Year 2 Depreciation = USD 75,000 x 25% = USD 18,750

Depreciation account of the balance sheet will look like below over the 8 years of the machine's life:

Year	Book Value at the beginning of the year (USD)	Depreciation (USD)	Book Value at the end of the year (USD)
1	100,000	25,000	75,000
2	75,000	18,750	56,250

3	56,250	14,063	42,188
4	42,188	10,547	31,641
5	31,641	7,910	23,730
6	23,730	5,933	17,798
7	17,798	4,449	13,348
8	13,348	2,348	**11,000**

e. _Sinking fund method_ – This method is also known as Depreciation Fund Method
or Redemption Fund Method. This method is based on the assumption that a fund is to be built up and that the amount of this fund should equal the total amount of the depreciation at the end of the useful life of the depreciable asset. An equal amount by way of depreciation is set aside by charging to the profit and Loss Account at the end of every accounting period, so that, all such equal installments if allowed to accumulate at a compound interest would equal to the depreciable cost of the asset at the expiry of its useful life.

Under all other methods of depreciation liquid cash may not be available to the firm at the time of asset replacement because in those cases the amount of depreciation is retained in the business. In this method, an equal installment is set off as depreciation is regularly invested outside the business in interest bearing and easily marketable securities. Interest yielded on such securities is compounded or reinvested in each year. When the life of the asset expires, investments are disposed off and the proceeds are utilized for replacing the old asset.

Formula
- Let's assume d = Sinking Fund Depreciation, C = Cost of the asset, S = Salvage value, i = Rate of interest in decimal term, n = Years.

$$d_a = \frac{(C - S).\, i}{[(1 + i)\,{}^{\wedge}n] - 1}$$

Example 9:

A machine costs USD 300,000 with a salvage value of USD 50,000 at the end of its life of 10 years. If it is worth 6% annually, use the sinking fund method to determine the depreciation at the 6th year. [24]

17

Solution

Annual depreciation, $d = \dfrac{(300{,}000 - 50{,}000) \times 0.06}{[(1.06)^{\wedge}10] - 1}$

$d = 18{,}966.98$

Depreciation after 6 years, $d_6 = \dfrac{d\,(1 + i)^{\wedge}n - 1)}{i}$

$d_6 = \dfrac{18{,}966.98\,(1.06)^{\wedge}6 - 1)}{0.06}$

$d_6 =$ USD 132,300.73

Note:

✓ There are quite a number of accounting methods that can be used to establish various asset values for many purposes including taxation, making investment decisions, rent fixation, mortgaging, mergers among others. These may not necessarily provide an accurate value of the reinstatement or replacement value of the asset for insurance purposes.

✓ In most valuation cases, the scrap/salvage value s assumed to be zero.

✓ Different depreciation methods can be applied as follows;

- o When consumption is constant over the useful life of the asset — Apply the straight-line method
- o When consumption is greater in the early years and less in the later years —Apply the declining balance method
- o When consumption increases as the asset approaches the end of its useful life—Apply the output method as explained in the following sections
- o When consumption varies with outputs/service—Apply the units of production method as explained in the following sections.

4.0 POLICY CATEGORIES & VALUATION

During business valuation, the valuer is required to have all the relevant facts and or documents to make a correct estimate of the asset values. These include purchase invoices, receipts & other product movement documents, taxation documents, asset life span journals among others. Below are some of the basis of valuation in some policies.

4.1 Goods in Transit / Marine

The term Goods in Transit refers to cargo that has been shipped or sent by the seller, but not yet received by the buyer.[12]

  a. Inland transit valuation – This simply means goods transported away from the coast within an area or region or within a territorial limit. The basis for the sum insured is usually the invoice or purchase cost value, plus any incidental costs to the insured that are not covered by the invoice. These might include transport charges, loading and offloading charges among others. If there are no invoice values, the valuation basis is the market value of the items.

b. <u>Marine</u> – This basically involves goods carried overseas. The sum Insured is the maximum amount of liability of the Insurer under the policy and is the measure of indemnity for a total loss. Usually the sum Insured is for the same amount as the Insured value on a one-off shipment but, this can differ on open policies where the sum Insured is shown as the maximum for any one vessel or conveyance or Insurers maximum liability and the actual shipment being declared is for the actual Insured value.

The basis of sum insured or valuation normally includes the main cost of the goods which is converted at the customs exchange rate plus insurance charges, freight customs duty, customs VAT, clearing charges and local transport costs. Additionally, the Insured is permitted to add a percentage (between 10% and 50%) to the total of the above charges. The added percentage is a provision for currency or exchange fluctuation, increase freight and or clearing charges in the event that the Insured has to re-order for the lost or damaged goods.

Indemnity/Value at Risk

When computing the value at risk, the purchase documents including the commercial invoice and other related charges and costs are reviewed to ascertain whether the declared sum insured was correct. If the value at risk is higher the sum insured, the loss is computed on Pro-rate basis which is the same as applying the average condition. If the VAR is less than the sum insured, the insured sums are adequate.

Example 10

Given the Inland Goods in Transit (GIT) policy which provides cover to the Insured's consignment of fish, fish maws and any other related to their business within USA on the items below:

- Limit per single transit: USD 37,837.84
- Estimated Annual Transit: USD 2,162,162.16

- Policy Basis of Valuation: Cost + Transport costs (Goods inwards and out wards) within Uganda.

Find the value at risk of the consignment which experienced an accident during transit to the Airport.

Solution

From the submitted documents, the total consignment value was noted to be USD 41,001.94 inclusive of freight and profit margin. The Insured provided us with a breakdown of their freight (via air), and profit charges which were estimated at 2.5% and 10% respectively. Their average inland transport charges for a single trip were estimated at USD 27.03. As such, the Value at Risk to computed as follows;

Total consignment value	:	USD 41,001.94
Less air freight charges (2.5%)	:	USD 3,075.15 (loss happened before)
Less profit margin (10%)	:	USD 2,300.58 (Buyer did not receive them)
Add Transport cost	:	USD 27.03
Value at Risk	:	**USD 25,653.24**

Example 11:

Cost Insurance Freight (C.I.F.) + 10% or more – mainly used for export shipments. Landed Cost to final destination + 10% (costs of the goods, freight charges, customs duty, customs VAT, clearing charges and local transportation costs). Freight and clearing charges appear on the Clearing Agents Invoice. Rate of exchange appears of the Customs Worksheet. Selling Price – mainly used on local sales. Invoice Value – mainly used for local purposes.

Calculate the Landed Cost of the goods.

Cost of Goods	= USD165 000
Sea freight	= USD 14 850
Cost + Freight	= USD 179 850
Customs Duty	= USD 49 500
Customs VAT	= USD 24 750
Clearing & Forwarding Charges	= USD 11 695
Landed Cost to final destination	= USD 265 795
Plus 10%	= USD 26 579
Total Sum Insured or VAR	= USD 292 374

Example 12:

Sum insured	= USD 200,000
Value at risk	= USD 350,000
Claim amount	= USD 75,000
Assessed amount	= USD 50,000
Average clause	= (Sum insured/value at risk) x Assessed amount
	= (200,000/350,000) x 50,000
After average	= USD 28,571.43 (Subject to the relevant policy provisions)

4.2 Money or Cash in Transit

A business may be robbed of cash either during normal business hours or after. Cash may be stolen whilst in transit between the bank and the office or on any other route. Money insurance usually covers loss of cash in transit, cash in the safe and can include theft or fire loss or damages to some properties like the safe or strong room.

The insured is usually required to provide their daily cash reports/retail sales reports and the sums insured may be derived from the total cash handled on a monthly and annual basis. They should also provide information regarding the maximum amount of cash in safe and transit and any one time. These policies are sometimes extended to cover properties including fixtures & fittings, computers and safes and strong room among other assets.

Indemnity/ value at risk

At the time of loss, the insured is required to provide the above documents among others depending the claim scenario, which indicate the amount of cash in their possession at the time of loss. In case this value is lower, this implies that the sum insured is adequate. On the other hand, if the VAR is higher than the sum insured, this implies under insurance and the insured is only covered up to the insured limit. The advised VAR also helps the insurer to negotiate for more premium during the next period of cover in case it was under declared in the previous policy. Regarding the insured fixtures & fittings, safes among other physical assets, the average condition or proportionate loss calculation usually applies incase the VAR for these items is found to be greater than the sum insured.

Example 13

An insurance client woke up one morning with an intention of banking some of the business cash at one of the popular banks in town. He first passed via his Hardware shop and collected the previous day sales and drove off to the bank using a motor cycle. As he approached the bank, his bike was suddenly kicked into the trench by another cyclist who immediately approached him and grabbed his bag within a blink of an eye. The victim or Insured sustained wounds after falling on his head in the trench and first went for medication before reporting the matter to police and insurance. They had also reported a robbery at their offices a few months ago.

During the loss assessment, the Insured presented documents which proved that he had USD 67,500 in his bag at the time of loss. Unfortunately, his money policy limit was USD 3,000 per event and was unable to recover the balance from the culprits who could not be traced

Regarding the office robbery, the sum insured against the safes, computers and other assets amounted to USD 5,000. The purchase invoice and market value of the vandalized doors, safe and computers indicated their VAR of USD 8,120, implying that these were also under insured, thus the application of 62% on the assessed loss of these items subject to the other relevant policy provisions like policy excess and salvage value etc.

4.3 Fidelity Guarantee

This covers any loss caused by forgery, embezzlement, larceny or fraudulent conversion of monies or stock in trade, whether belonging to the Insured or held in trust by him- committed by the employed person in connection with his employment as specified in the policy. The indemnity provided is for the amount of money lost or for the value of lost items comprising such loss to the limit of the respective sums Insured applicable against the name of the employee (in case of an individual or collective policy) or to the limit of the aggregate amount of guarantee.

Sum insured & value at risk

Choosing the right sums or limits can be achieved by establishing the maximum cash handled by specific individuals and aggregate amount established by reviewing the maximum amount that the insured may lose due to the fraudulent acts of their staff including connivance. At the time of Loss, the insured is only covered up to the limit of their sum insured even when the value at risk is higher than the declared sum. In this case the value at risk is difficult to estimate/

establish as majority of insurers rely on the declared sums. Some rely the amounts of cash or value of goods that their staff (s) handle in a given period.

Example 14

A certain firm manager wanted to purchase a fidelity guarantee policy for his staff. Since he did not have enough funds to take cover on a blanket basis, he decided to be specific to those staff members that handle the business cash and these were his 2 accountants and 3 cashiers at a total sum insured of USD 50,000. After about 6 months, one of the cashiers disappeared with USD 74,360 which he was required to bank and the claim was paid up to the limit of the sum insured less excess and other policy provisions.

4.4 Burglary /Robbery

This policy usually covers losses or damages to the Insured property as a result forced entry. The sum Insured here is either on a full value basis and or first loss basis. Full value basis means the policyholder is insuring their property based on the actual value of the property or items. This basis is adopted if there is a high possibility of the entire property being stolen at any one time. First loss basis means you are insuring the maximum probable theft loss at any one time. This basis is adopted if it is highly impossible for the entire Insured property being stolen at any one time.

Sum insured & value at risk

The sum insured is usually based on the asset purchase costs plus relevant charges for reinstating the same if applicable. The policyholder can submit this information through their asset register which would indicate the cost, purchase date and depreciated price of the assets. The basis of compensation for all affected items can be based on the purchase price and or market value (which may include a depreciation or reinstatement value basis.[16] At the time of loss, the VAR may be establishing by reviewing the asset purchase invoices or asset register or conducting independent market inquiries into the lost or damaged items. In case the VAR of the assets in greater that the sums insured, then policyholder bears a proportionate share of the loss accordingly. Regarding the cash in the premises, this is usually covered up to the limit of the sum insured.

Example 15

A group of thugs broke through a client's forex bureau in the night. They had rented a nearby shop that had recently been vacated by a tenant. The thugs had spent some time studying the client's business and building security and eventually slept over during the weekend and broke through the client's business through a wall and took cash amounting to USD 30,000. They also vandalized other properties like the safe, strong room, CCTV and computers worth USD 10,000.

The sums insured for the cash and property were USD 20,000 and USD 50,000 respectively. From the submitted documents, the VAR for these items was noted to be USD 30,000 and USD 75,000 respectively. Regarding the stolen cash, the maximum limit or sum insured was considered as the assessed amount. A proportionate loss of 20% was applied to the assessed loss for the vandalized or stolen property in view of the under insurance of this item. The total assessed amount was then subjected to relevant policy provisions.

4.5 Public Liability

Public Liability cover is a policy that protects against claims of personal injury or property damage that a third party suffers as a result of the Insured's business activities. These claims could be made by clients, contractors, or members of the public for accidental injury or damage to their property and could arise from an incident on the business premises or as a result of the business operations. The public liability cover may include consideration of the following factors that may determine the extent of compensation for any damages;

- ✓ Size of the business
- ✓ Neighborhood and business activities
- ✓ Level of interaction with the public
- ✓ Type of clients
- ✓ Scale of contracts
- ✓ Claims and or hazard history
- ✓ Geographical location and terrain
- ✓ Business operations
- ✓ The level of risk associated with the industry among other factors

Sum insured & value at risk

The sum insured is meant to include amounts payable, inclusive of any legal costs recoverable from the insured by a claimant or any number of claimants and all other costs and expenses incurred with the insurer's consent for any event or series of events with one original cause or source. This does not exceed the limit of indemnity or sum insured. This can be best estimated by first identifying the business risks in relation to the clients and other 3rd parties and then estimating the maximum amount that would be lost in settling their potential claims or losses. In this case the value at risk is difficult to estimate/ establish as majority of insurers rely on the declared sums or limit for each insured item under the policy.

Example 16

A certain building under construction suddenly collapsed to the ground close to a parking area and caused damage to four vehicles therein. It also collapsed into a nearby super market shop and damaged a number of items therein. The supermarket and vehicle owners sued the building owner who referred them to his contractor. The claimants wanted compensations amounting to USD 1,456,858. Unfortunately, the contractor's limit was at USD 500,000. Contractor ended up being their own Insurer for the uninsured sum.

4.6 Products Liability

Product liability cover protects the business from claims related to medical costs, compensatory damages, economic damages, and in some instances, attorneys' fees, costs and punitive damages. It covers the manufacturer's or seller's liability for losses or injuries to a buyer, user or bystander caused by a defect or malfunction of the product, and, in some instances, a defective design or a failure to warn.

There are generally three types of products "claims" a company may face:

- ✓ Manufacturing or Production Flaws. A claim that some part of the production process created an unreasonably unsafe defect in the resulting product.
- ✓ Design Defect. A claim that the design of the product is inherently unsafe.
- ✓ Defective Warnings or Instructions. A claim that the product was not properly labeled or had insufficient warnings for the consumer to understand the risk.

Sum insured & value at risk

The sums insured & premiums on such policies maybe based on the type of product, volume of sales, and the role of the Insured in the process.[18] Choosing a limit may also depend on the nature of the product, lifespan or expiry date and effected if taken in expired state among other factors. The valuer or surveyor should in this case consider a worst-case scenario arising from a given product and estimate the cost of settling the claim(s) including any legal fees and losses that could be incurred by the policyholder as a result of the incident. Similarly, the value at risk here is difficult to estimate/ establish as majority of insurers rely on the declared sums or limit for each insured item under the policy.

Example 17

A certain fuel station experienced a heavy rain in the night that resulted into floods that accessed their underground fuel tanks and contaminated the various petroleum products therein. The policyholder thought that the rain water had not accessed the tank areas and served about 75 customers very early that morning and later received complaints from these vehicles which broke down in the courses of their journeys. The fuel station was held liable for these damages.

Their sum insured was USD 100,000. However, each claimant requested for about USD 2,500 to restore their vehicles engines & related parts from these damages thus leading to a total claim of USD 187,500. The Insurer only paid up to the insured policy limit of USD 100,000 and the policyholder was their own insurer for the un insured part of the loss.

4.7 Workman's Compensation (WCO)

This policy is mandatory of all employers under the state laws and covers injuries or accidents sustained by employees during the course of their employment duties. An injured staff can file a workman's compensation claim and receive weekly payments to cover medical bills or lost wages. This may also cover diseases contracted or arising out of and in the course of employment works. There are usually two broad approaches of arriving at the compensations rates as shown below; [17]

✓ Average Weekly Wage. Under this approach, employees get a percentage of their average weekly wage depending on regulations from the state workers' compensation insurance.

✓ Partial vs Total Disability. The weekly amount for the employees is also based on the type of injury or illness they have. If they're partially or totally disabled, they'll get different benefts than someone with a temporary injury. In fact. a totally disabled employee will typically get 60% or 2/3 of their average weekly wage. Each state or condition also has a maximum weekly rate. It is therefore important understand the rules and benefit amount for each condition or state.

Sum insured & value at risk

The sum insured and value ct risk is based on the payroll or list of all the present staff members and their salaries at a given time. if the number of employees (whether on duty or otherwise) employed by the insured on the date of accident is higher than the number covered under the policy, the Insurer indemnifies, only in such proportion that the number of employees covered bears to the employees found employed on the dcte of accident.

If the amount of wages declared for all employees is less than the actual wages paid until date of acciden-, the Insurer only indemnifies in proportion of -he wages declared to the wages paid. Wages declared can be calculated proportionately from the period from commencement of policy until date of accident for compcrison with the actual wages paid during such period to determine applicabil ty of th s clause.

If the liability of the insured for any clair by an employee is determined on the basis of wages and s higher than one covered under the policy, the Insurer is liable to indemnify only a proportion of the wages covered by the policy which the employee/employees bear(s) to the wages on the basis of which insured is held liable. In this case, the wages covered in respect of any employee snall represent the average wage per employee in the category under which the employee falls as specified in the schedule, unless actual wages paid at the time of accident is substantiated by submission of documentary evidence to the Insurer.

Example 18: Establishing the annual and weekly wage.

A full-time employee made USD 50,000 last year afte- working for 242 days. If USD 50,000 is divided by 242, her average daily wage is USD 206.61. Next, multiply USD 206.61 by 260 (the number of days she wou d work in a year). That should equal USD 53,718.60. Finally, divide USD 53,718.60 by 52 (the number of weeks in a year), to get

---

her average weekly wage of USD 1,033.05.

Example 19: Computing John's compensation.

If John's Average Weekly Wage (AWW) is USD 900, his compensation rate is 2/3 of that i.e. USD 600. If he chooses to be paid weekly over 500 weeks, he will ultimately receive USD 600 x 500 weeks= USD 300,000.

Example 20:

- Sum insured (wages)   = USD 100,000
- Value at Risk (wages)   = USD 500,000
- Claim amount   = USD 70,000
- Assessed amount   = USD 45,000
- Average   = (Sum insured/Value at risk) x Assessed amount
                           = (100,000 / 500,000) x 45,000
- After average   = USD 9,000 (subject to policy terms & conditions)

4.8 Group Personal Accident (GPA)

Group Personal Accident policies are usually taken by employers and or special staff members including directors, managers, accountants among others. They compensate the staff against bodily injury, solely and directly caused by accidental, violent, visible and external means, during the period of cover and result in death, partial or permanent disability and medical expenses even when they are not performing their employment duties. The policy may be on a named, department or unnamed basis and may be computed according to the state laws.

Basis of the Sum insured

Generally, the practice is that the sum insured is derived at three to five times of the annual salary of the Insured Person. The following is just a guide for deriving the sum insured;

No.	Item Description	Comment
1	Accidental Death	The Insured is free to choose any amount as the capital sum insured but not more than 5 times of the Insured's annual income.
2	Permanent Total Disablement	As above plus 25% of Capital Sum Insured if the

		insured requires constant assistance of another person on permanent basis
3	Permanent Partial Disablement	As per percentages set out in Act of periodic earrings e.g. monthly
4	Temporary Total Disablement - per week	The amount to be insured under this benefit is based on 75% of weekly income
5	Temporary Partial Disablement - per week	The amount to be insured under this benefit is 50% of Temporary Total Disability
6	Medical expenses, funeral, transport & incidental costs, repatriation of mortal remains, modification of residence, recruitment expense benefit, airfares for treatment etc.	The Insured is free to choose the limits for each of these items hereunder separately. Usually it range from 5% to 10% of the capital sum insured

Indemnity/Value at risk

At the time of loss, all the staff's employment records including their salaries are reviewed from which the adequacy of the above tabulated estimated limits are checked. If they are found to be greater than the declared sums, the Insurer only pays up to the Insured limit for each loss or claim item. The insured can later be advised to upgrade these limits so as to enjoy more benefits.

Example 21

A Group Personal Policy was issued to 4 employees whose names were also stated. One of the them called Peter (Site Engineer & Supervisor), was delivering some site materials and cash when he suddenly landed into a group of thugs who kicked his motorcycle and mugged him. They not only took his personal belonging but also took cash that was supposed to be delivered to the site.

During the claim assessment, he provided all the medical expenses that he incurred to recover from the injuries and these amounted to USD 12,000 and this amount was well substantiated. Unfortunately, the policy limit for the medical expenses was USD 6,000 and this was the compensation that peter received.

Example 22

A mezzanine floor caved in and caused the death of one of the factory accountants. The GPA policy was as follows;

No.	Position	No. Persons	Sum Insured (USD)
1	Director	1	20,000

2	Marketing	1	20,000
3	Accountants @ USD 20,000	2	40,000
4	Expatriates, Senior managers, Supervisors, Administrators Engineers @ 10,000	15	150,000
Total			230,000

During the claim computation, the employment records for the deceased were reviewed and his 60 months' earnings (from his monthly salary x 5) amounted to USD 35,000. Therefore, this item was noted to be underinsured his next of kins only received the limit of USD 20,000.

4.9 Professional Indemnity

Professional Indemnity insurance protects professionals against claims of negligence or breach of duty made by a client as a result of receiving misleading professional advice or services. It is usually applied in scenarios were the policyholder is or are alleged to have provided misleading or inadequate advice, services or designs to a client and also provides cover for the legal costs and expenses in defending the claim as well as compensation payable to your client to rectify the mistake. Regardless of how many years or experience a company may have, there is always the possibility of a mistake. Professional indemnity insurance may cover against a wide range of scenarios, including: [20]

✓ Professional negligence (i.e. making a mistake in a task/service for a client)
✓ Loss of documents or data
✓ Unintentional breach of copyright and/or confidentiality
✓ Defamation and libel

Sum insured & Value at Risk

Choosing a professional indemnity insurance limit depends on the policyholder's business operations were there may be high chances of making an error or mistake. The valuer or surveyor should in this case consider a worst-case scenario arising from a certain business operation or activity and basing on the size of the business to estimate the cost of putting it right and including any legal fees and losses that could be incurred by your client as a result of the error. Since the policy holder understands their business risks better, the value at risk here is difficult to estimate/ establish as majority of insurers rely on the declared sums or limits for each insured item under the policy.

Example 23

A certain bank was reportedly robbed by an unknown thug who targeted their old ATM machines. The fraud star had studied the ATMs for some time and equipped himself with the necessary master keys and malware which he had used to disrupt the machine systems and command them to print money. He also took advantage of the fact that the bank ATM rooms were always closed and security could not easily interfere with clients in the ATM rooms. The cameras in the ATM could not capture his face because he was wearing a cap.

The thug took USD 40,000, USD 12,000, 56,000 and 39,000 from the bank ATMs thus leading to a total event loss of USD 147,000. The bank chose to blame the respective ATM guards at the various branches who were not seen anyway close to the ATM during the robbery. Others security officers were seen conversing with their fellow guards while the robbery was taking place. Unfortunately, the security company policy limit for professional indemnity had a limit of USD 100,000 per event and this is what they received less the policy excess. The security company was now required to pay the uninsured sum until the loss was fully recovered.

4.10 Business Interruption

Business interruption insurance (BI) is also known as time loss, consequential loss and loss of profits insurance. It usually provides cover for the financial losses due to an interruption to a business caused by material damage to property. Typical Business Interruption policies usually cover gross profit or gross revenue and increased cost of working and or savings. Others may be extended to cover expenses like fixed costs and wages.

The indemnity period starts at the date of damage and ends when the business is no longer affected by it, or when the end of the Maximum Indemnity Period is reached. The actual period affected is known as the Indemnity Period and the Maximum Indemnity Period is the point at which the policy ceases to respond.

Gross profit is the term that Insurers use for the addition of net profit and standing charges. Standing charges are also known as fixed expenses. The gross profit is calculated by deducting variable expenses (uninsured working expenses) from the turnover. The figures are adjusted for differences between opening and closing stock.

The increased cost of working caters for extra expenses to stabilize the business following a loss and may include such as renting alternative premises, hiring additional staff, additional advertising, subcontracting or arranging overtime working among other expenses. [22]

32

Sum insured & value at risk

The sums insured are usually derived from the financial records submitted by the insured including audited financial statements, profit & loss statements, sales records, expense records among others. During a claim, the same are reviewed to ascertain the value at risk. If the policy is not declaration linked and the Value at risk for the loss of gross profit is greater than the sum insured, this calls for the application of the average clause after computing the total assessed amount including the increased cost of working and savings.

Example 24:

Below is an illustration of how to arrive at the insurable gross profit which is the sum of your turnover, closing stock & work in progress (derived from the business at the Insured's premises), less the sum of your opening stock & work in progress. The Insured can sometimes eliminate expenses that they do not want to insure for purposes of reducing on the premium. All this information is derived from various business records provided by the Insured.

Total Turnover/Sales
Plus, Closing Stock & Work in Progress
Less Opening Stock & Work in Progress
Sub Total A (Turnover)
Less *Total uninsured expenses* (Expenses you don't want to insure or not insured) i.e.
      Purchases of Consumables, Stock, etc.
      Commissions
      Freight & Packaging
      Wages
      Subcontractor, Labour hire
Subtotal B (Insurable gross profit)

Plus, adjustment for trend of business since last accounting period @ (%)
Plus, adjustment for trend of business during policy period @ (%)
Plus, adjustment for trend of business during indemnity period @ (%)

The Insurable Gross Profit for a 12-month Indemnity Period is attained by multiplying the above by Multiply the above by;
a) 150% for an 18-month Indemnity Period
b) 200% for a 24-month Indemnity Period
c) 300% for a 36-month Indemnity Period

The Insured Rate of Gross Profit is (Sub Total B divide Sub Total A)
Additional increased cost of working (minimum 10% of Sub Total A)

Example 25:

The insured's policy has a sum insured on loss of gross profit of USD 150,000 and Indemnity period of 12 months. Their premises experienced an earthquake on 1/01/2020, and it took 12 months to restore the business. The turnover for 2019 was USD 1,000,000, 2018 was USD 1,200,000 and 2016 was USD 900,000. Rate of gross profit in the same period prior or previous year is 40%. Actual turnover during the indemnity period is assumed to USD 350,000. Other factors constant, compute the Value at Risk for the gross profit.

Solution

Since the turnover of 2018 is greater than that of 2019, implies a downward trend in the turnover i.e.

- 2018 – USD 1,200.000
- 2019 – USD 1,000.000
  USD 200.000

Therefore, the downward trend s computed as (200,000 /1,200,000) x 100% = -16.67%

Standard turnover from 1/01/2019 to 1/12/2019 = USD 1,000,000
Trend (say -16.67% of standard turnover) = USD 166,668
Actual turnover = USD 350,000
Loss or reduction in turnover 2020 = USD 483,333

Loss of gross profit = 483,333 X 40% = USD 193,333

This also implies a Value at Risk of USD 193,333 indicating under insurance at USD 150,000 which calls for the application of the average clause after computing the total assessed amount f the policy is not declaration linked

4.11 Contractor All Risks (CAR) & Erection All Risks (EAR)

The basic concept of CAR or EAR cover is to provide the contractor and or subcontractor protection for physical loss or damage happening at the construction/ erection site caused by perils which are not specifically excluded by these policies. These also cover liabilities arising from 3rd parties which may include 3rd party property damage or bodily injury arising in connection with the execution of the project. The cover normally starts from the commencement of the project works and may extend to include the testing and maintenance periods.

CAR coverage is mainly used for construction or civil engineering projects like buildings, roads, bridges etc. and may include cover for other electrical and or mechanical project works which for part of the sum insured. EAR coverage is mainly for erection installing of machinery and equipment which may not be limited to power lines, elevators, plumbing systems, installation of plant & machinery or structures, wiring equipment, stabilizers among other electrical or mechanical fixtures and fittings.

Sum insured & Value at risk

The sums insured are usually derived from the project valuations which are normally indicated in the project contract between the employer and main contractor. The value at risk for the contract works is usually obtained by comparing the insured sum and the actual value in the contract/agreement using the exchange rates and approved construction or erection rates in the contract. This should be equal to the value in the contract as well as sum insured. If this is greater than the sum insured, this implies under insurance and the insured only receives a proportionate portion of their loss. However, this does not apply to the third-party losses which are usually covered up to the insured limit.

Note:

- ✓ Sometimes the Value at Risk for the CAR/ EAR may continuously decline depending on the progress of the project. For example, in a road construction project, the insured may choose to reduce the sum insured by reducing the value of the completed works which have exceeded the testing the period and are already in use since these policies may sometimes cease to cover such works.
- ✓ Usually these project contracts have Bills of Quantities (BOQ) that form the basis of these agreements and these may include the cost of procuring materials from the supplier, freight and erection costs.
- ✓ The valuation basis generally depends on the policy wording.

Example 26

A certain hotel project was insured at USD 1,200,000. The material damage claim under the Contractors All Risks policy amounted to USD 300,000.

At the time of loss, the policyholder was required to provide a number of documents which included its BOQ and project agreement or contract. Upon review of the same, the actual project value in the contract was noted to be USD 5,970,000 implying that there was gross underinsurance hence the application of the average clause. The assessed loss was noted to be USD 250,000 and the average was applied as follows.

Average   clause   = (Sum insured/Value at risk) x Assessed amount
                     = (1,200,000 / 5,970,000) x 250,000
After average   = USD 50,251.26 (subject to policy terms & conditions)

Example 27

During a road construction project on a steep slope, a number of third parties were affected by the construction machine excavations and vibrations. The area also experienced heavy rains that caused flooding in the neighborhoods since the contractor was not yet through with the drainage channel construction thus leading to a number of third party loses.

Upon review of the policy, the sum insured against the 3rd party losses was USD 10,000, yet the policy holder's or contractors claim was USD 37,500. They only received the insured limit i.e. 10,000 and were their own insurer for the rest of the loss.

5.0 OFFICE EQUIPMENT & HOUSE HOLD ITEMS

The value for office equipment or household items can be attained by use of valuation methods. These include among others the comparison method and book value method.

5.1 Comparison approach.

Under this approach, the valuer notes down the specifications of the relevant item. The valuer should choose an item with similar specifications or all almost all specification in order to the attain an accurate replacement value/ market value of an item. These specifications are compared with those of local and foreign dealers in consideration of the other factors like freight and taxes. Alternatively, if the valuer has a data base of similar items which they have previously valued, this could also form the basis of establishing the market value.

Example 28

Peter was assigned to value a certain company's office equipment below. The insured was interested in knowing their market value for insurance purposes as well as the disposal values.

- 87 chairs	- 4 desktops
- 23 tables	- 7 32-inch flat screens
- 20 cabinets	- 18 other equipment
- 20 laptops	

Solution

Peter visited the company, inspected the items and noted down their respective specifications. He later visited various suppliers of similar products and noted down their replacement values. Since the client wanted to insure their property as is. Peter applied different depreciations rates to the different items to account for their period in use and physical condition at the time of inspection. A flat disposal rate of 30% was adopted since most of the items had been in use for the same period.

No.	Description	Repl. Value (USD)	Market values (USD)	Disposal value (USD)
1	Chairs	2,072.97	1,762.03	621.89
2	Tables	1,114.86	1,014.53	334.46
3	Bookshelves / Cabinets	864.86	769.73	259.46
4	Laptops	722.97	592.84	216.89
5	CPUs	86.49	77.84	25.95
6	Monitor	13.51	13.51	4.05
7	Keyboards	8.11	8.11	2.43
8	Television sets	2,297.30	1,722.97	689.19
9	Other equipment	754.05	588.16	226.22
	Total	7,935	6,550	2,381

5.2 Book value approach

In this method, the client can avail/submit the purchase invoices or receipts for the various household items under consideration. An appropriate depreciation rate can be applied to establish their estimated market value.

Sum insured & value at risk

The sum insured is usually on replacement or indemnity basis depending on the policy wording and is usually based on the declared values by the insured. At the time of loss, the value at risk may be attained by acquiring an updated asset register of the insured's office equipment and establishing their cost or market values. If the value of risk is greater than the sum insured and the 85% average and or appraisement clause are not applicable, then average clause shall apply.

Example 29:

Sum insured	= USD 100,000
Value at risk	= USD 160,000
Claim amount	= USD 47,000
Assessed amount	= USD 30,000

Average clause = (Sum insured/Value at risk) x Assessed amount
= (100,000 / 160,000) x 30.000
After average = USD 18,750 (subject to policy terms & conditions)

6.0 STOCK IN TRADE

Stock in trade in this case includes physical agricultural and industrial stocks and can be categorized into raw materials, work in progress and finished goods. These stock values can be established by making use of the stock records. In absence of these records, the valuer may need to adopt other approaches which may assist in estimating the stock quantities and then use the prevailing market prices to compute their values.

6.1 Stock records approach

Stock records provided by the Insured may include the stock movement records, periodic stock takes or tally sheets and stocks valuation records, purchase invoices among others.

Note:

- ✓ Since stock companies usually conduct periodic stock valuations to estimate the values of their stocks, the same could be availed to aid in computing the Value at Risk especially the last valuations close to the date of loss.
- ✓ Alternatively, the insured can submit all the documents relating to the stocks present at the time of loss and the value at risk can be computed from the same as illustrated in the examples below.

Example 30:

A company experienced a damage to their agricultural stocks on 12/08/2014. The reportedly affected stocks include unprocessed cocoa (3 MT), coffee (42 MT), maize (1.7 MT), soya beans (1.2 MT). The entire stocks in the factory included all the above in the categories of raw materials, semi-finished goods and processed goods. Find the value at risk of the stocks.

Solution

Unit costs on 12/08/2014

Unprocessed	Semi-finished goods	Processed/ finished goods
- Cocoa – USD 0.5 per Kg - Coffee – USD 1.5 per Kg - Maize – USD 0.2 per Kg - Soya beans – USD 0.3 per Kg	- Cocoa – USD 0.7 per Kg - Coffee – USD 1.7 per Kg - Maize – USD 0.4 per Kg - Soya beans – USD 0.5 per Kg	- Cocoa – USD 1.5 per Kg - Coffee – USD 2.5 per Kg - Maize – USD 0.8 per Kg - Soya beans – USD 1 per Kg

Overall stock quantities as at 12/08/2014 in Metric Tons (MT)

Unprocessed (MT)	Semi-finished goods (MT)	Processed/ finished goods (MT)
- Cocoa – 200 MT - Coffee – 910 MT - Maize – 304 MT - Soya beans – 215 MT	- Cocoa – 74 MT - Coffee – 156 MT - Maize – 98 MT - Soya beans – 69 MT	- Cocoa – 135 MT - Coffee – 567 MT - Maize – 213 MT - Soya beans – 178 MT

Overall stock Valuation /Value at Risk as at 12/08/2014 is **USD 3,749,400** as tabulated below:

Unprocessed (USD)	Semi-finished goods (USD)	Processed/ finished goods (USD)
- Cocoa – 100,000 - Coffee – 1,365,000 - Maize – 60,800 - Soya beans – 64,500	- Cocoa – 51,800 - Coffee – 265,200 - Maize – 39,200 - Soya beans – 34,500	- Cocoa – 202,500 - Coffee – 1,417,500 - Maize – 170,400 - Soya beans – 178,000

Example 31

Given the information in the table below, Find the value of stock as on 31/03/2012 given that the gross profit earned during the year from 31/03/2011 is 20% of sales.[30]

No.	Item description	Amount (USD)
1	Stock as on 1/04/2011	22,000
2	Purchases	52,500
3	Manufacturing Expenses	30,000
4	Selling Expenses	12,100
5	Administration Expenses	6,000
6	Financial Expenses	4,300
7	Sales	240,000

At the time of valuing stock as on 31/03/2011, the gross profit earned during the year was 20% on sales.
Solution
Statement for stock valuation on 31/3/2012

Item	1/04/2011(USD)	31/03/2012 (USD)
Stock as on 1/04/2011	22,000	
Add: Expenses related to production		
- Purchases	152,500	
- Manufacturing expenses	30,000	
Total product + production expenses	**174,500**	
		By sales: 240,000
Less: Gross profit @ 20% of sales		Gross profit: 48,000
Total cost of sales		**192,000**
Value of Stock as on 31/03/2012		= 22,000+174,500-192,000 = 204,500-192,000 = **12,500**

Example 32

John prepares accounts on 30th September every year, but on 31/12/2011, a flood destroyed the greater part of his stock. T h e following information was collected from his records: [30]

No.	Item description	Amount (USD)
1	Stock as on 1/10/2011(beginning stock)	33,000
2	Purchases from 1/10/2011 to 31/12/2011	75,000
3	Wages from 1/10/2011 to 31/12/2011	33,000
4	Sales from 1/10/2011 to 31/12/2011	140,000

The rate of gross profit is 25% of sales. The salvage from the stock was U S D 3,000 was salvaged. The plant was installed by the company's own technician. He was paid USD 500, which was included in wages. Purchases include the purchase of the plant for USD 5,000. Calculate the value of stock on 31/12/2011.

Solution

Item	1/10/2011 (USD)	31/12/2011 (USD)
Opening stock	**33,000**	
Add: Expenses related to production		
- Purchases	75,000	
• Less: Cost of plant	-5,000	
- Wages	33,000	
• Less: Wages paid for plant	-500	
Total product + production expenses	**102,500**	
		By Sales: 140,000
Less: Gross profit @ 25% of sales		Gross profit: 35,000
Total cost of sales		**105,000**
By closing stock		= 33,000+102,500-105,00
		=135,500-105,000
		=30,500

6.2 Physical count approach

This involves a physical count of the stocks present at a given place and best applies for smaller stocks and or stocks that can easily be counted. It is quite tedious especially for clients with large stocks but may be applicable in scenarios were clients lacks the required stock records. To simplify this assignment, the valuer can make use of the stack cards of the various stocks to establish or estimate the various quantites of stock in a given warehouse. If these cards are missing, an interview with the stock manager could assist after which the valuer can sampe some of the availed information by physically counting some of stocks in the warehouses. This however requires the valuer to have or organize their data collection record to cater for the various quantities and types of stocks.

Note:

✓ During the stock loss claim, a physical count is the best approach especially if the stocks are still present or parially damaged and the assessor or adjuster is strongly encouraged to embark on this method as soon as they are appointed before the Insured tampers with any of the reportecly affected items either by adding some rejected stocks or disposing it off before its physically counted.

Example 33:

The Insured is a manufacturer of biscuits/ flour and reported a claim of floods that soaked all their stocks. Unfortunately, the soaked stocks started stinking thus the need for their immediate disposal. You are assigned to advise on the value at loss of the stock.

Solution

If need be, the valuer/ assessor can hire some casual workers, provide them with gloves and masks to aic in the counting process.

No.	Item	description	Tally	Qty (boxes)
1	Biscuit	Milk	11111111111111111111111111_11111111111111111111111111111111111 1111111111111111111111111111_11111111111111111111111111111111111111111 111111111111111111111111111_111111111111111111111111111111111 1111111111111111111111111111_11111111111111111111111111111111 1111111111111111111111111111_1111111111111111111111111111111111111111	4,889
2	Biscuit	Chocolate	111111111111111111111111111111111111111111111111111111111111111111 11111111111111111111111111111111111111111111111111111111111111111111 11111111111111111111111111111111111111111111	1,570
3	Biscuit	Letter type	11111111111111111111111111111111111111111111111111111111111111111 111111111111111111111111111111111111111111111111111111111111 1111111111111111111111111111111111111111111111111111111111111111 111111111111111111111111111111111111111111111111111111111111111111 1111111111111111111111111111111111111111111111111111111111	6,652
4	Biscuit	Round shape	1111111111111111111111111111111111111111111111111111111111111 111111111111111111111111111111111111111111111111111111111111111111111 111111111111111111111111111111111111111111111111111111111111111111 11111111111111111111111111111111111111111111111	47,487
5	Biscuit	Straw berry	111111111111111111111111111111111111111111111111111111111111 11111111111111111111111111111111111111111111111:111	522
6	Biscuit	Stick type	1111111111111111111111111111111111111111111111:1 1111111111111111111111111111111111111 1111111111111111111111111111111111111111111111:1111111111111111111111	740

After the tally and counting, the valuer uses the unit costs of each type which are profit margin and VAT exclusive to advise on the Value at Risk of the stocks.

Example 34:

The Insured's stock or grain in a silo and warehouse floor was affected by heavy rains that also caused flooding the grain warehouse. Unfortunately, the grain was already moisturized and beginning to cake thus the need for its quick valuation or assessment before disposing it off to potential salvage buyers. Assuming that all the stocks and grains in the silos or warehouses are affected.

Solution

Trucks of known carrying capacity can assist in the quantification exercise. These affected stocks are loaded onto these trucks which are required to pass via weighbridges were the stock weights are noted and printed. The weights can be clustered according to the extent of damage or grade rather than mixing them together. After adding up all the affected quantities, grades and value from the insured's records/advise, the adjuster can now have a basis for bargaining with potential salvage buyers.

6.3 Geometric approach

This involves taking measurements of the shape containing the affected stocks which may be a rectangular room or warehouses, cylindrical silos among others for purposes of computing the affected contents or quantities. It helps to compute the maximum quantity of stock that is covered in a given area or volume. During a claim, it can aid in computing the maximum quantities of damaged stock in a given silo, stack or warehouse.

Procedure for computing the value at risk.

- Equip yourself with a note book, tape measure and camera.
- Note the specifics of the affected stock i.e. its name and density among others.
- Measure the dimensions of the warehouse or silo or shape containing the stocks.
- Alternatively, draw a rough sketch of the initial positions of the stock stacks or shape or level of the stocks. Measure the dimensions of each box or PP bag containing stock or the weight of each PP bag for each type of affected stock.
- Acquire the necessary formulas to assist you in the calculation of object areas or volumes so as to obtain the maximum possible quantities of stocks and maximum affected quantities therein (after noting the level of damage).

- After attaining the maximum possible quantities, apply their unit costs to attain the total stock Value at Risk.

Example 35:

The Insured reported a claim where they lost over 40 Metric Tons (MT) of coffee that were in their 50 MT silo due to heavy rains that blew off a section of its top structure. The Insured substantiated their claim with stock documents leading to the claimed quantities. Find the value at risk of the stock in the silo.

Solution

Equip yourself with the necessary measurement tools that can assist you in attaining the height and diameter of the silo. The insured can sometimes provide these details. Some silos usually have stair cases that can be used to confirm the actual height of the affected stocks as illustrated below;

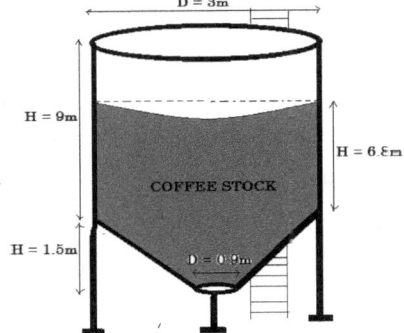

Maximum Silo coffee handling Capacity
Volume of the entire silo = Cylindrical shape volume + Cone shape volume

$$= \pi R^2 H + \frac{\pi H}{3} (R^2 + Rr + r^2)$$

$$= \pi \times (3/2)^2 \times 9 + \frac{\pi \times 1.5}{3} ((3/2)^2 + (3/2) \times (0.9/2) + (0.9/2)^2$$
$$= 63.62 + 4.91 = 68.53 \ m^3$$

Mass = Density of coffee x Volume of silo
$$= 561 \ kg/m^3 \times 68.53 \ m^3$$
$$= 38,445.33 \ Kg = \underline{38.45 \ MT} \ (Silo \ Capacity)$$

Maximum Possible Qty in Silo
Volume occupied by Coffee = Cylindrical volume portion + Cone shape volume

$$= \pi R^2 H + \frac{\pi H}{3} (R^2 + Rr + r^2)$$

$$= \pi \times (3/2)^2 \times 6.8 + \frac{\pi \times 1.5}{3} ((3/2)^2 + (3/2) \times (0.9/2) + (0.9/2)^2$$
$$= 43.066 + 4.91 = 52.98 \ m^3$$

Mass = 561 x 52.98 = 29,719.74 Kg = <u>29.72 MT</u>
Unit cost from original invoices of 1 kg of coffee = USD 1.14
Coffee value at loss = 29,719.74 x1.14 = <u>USD 33,735.92</u>

Note:

✓ In case the stocks were immediately disposed of before you were appointed. The approach can apply in situation were marks of the affected stocks heights are still existing on the silo or structures walls.

Example 36:

The policyholder reported a loss or damage to wheat Grain in their warehouse due to floods that accessed their store through the warehouse entrance and attained a height of 0.4 m from the ground level. Find the quantity and value of the damaged stock as shown below.

Actual shape	**Estimated for computation purposes**

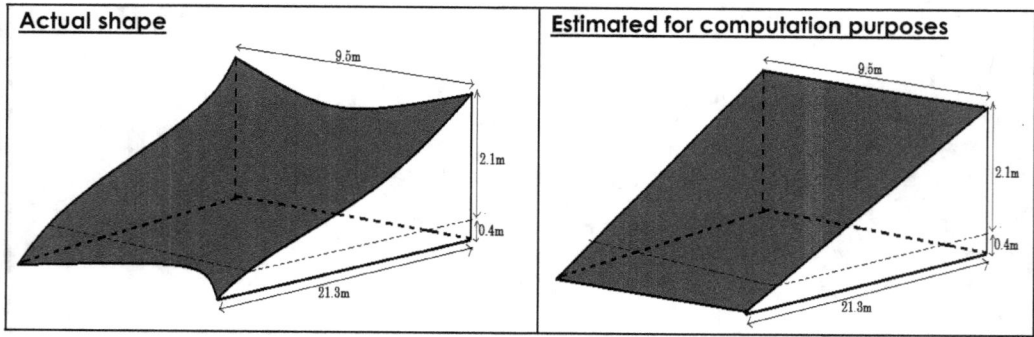

Solution

After measuring the same occupied by the affected stock and the maximum heights at the edges. The shape can be standardized to assist calculating the maximum possible quantities as shown below.

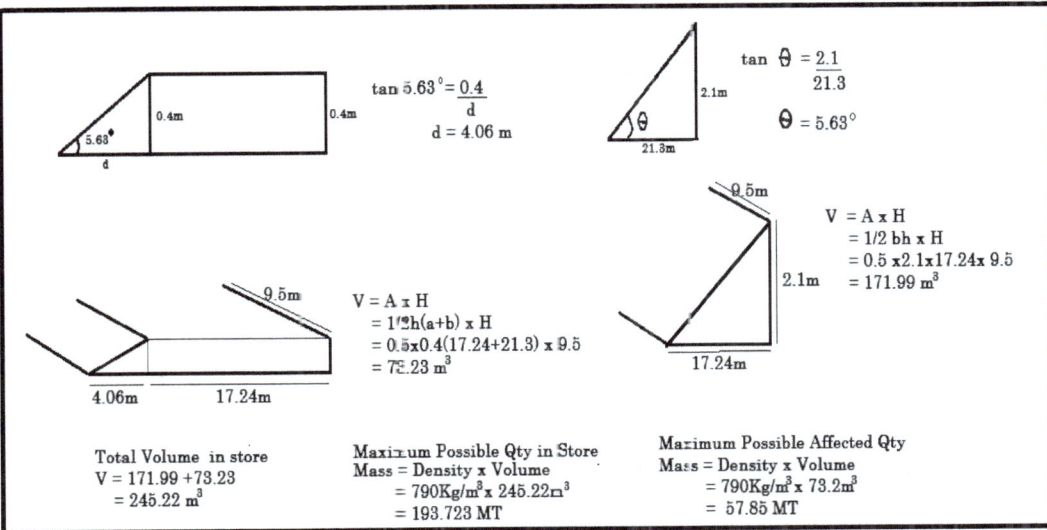

$$\tan 5.63° = \frac{0.4}{d}$$
$$d = 4.06 \text{ m}$$

$$\tan \theta = \frac{2.1}{21.3}$$
$$\theta = 5.63°$$

$$V = A \times H$$
$$= 1/2 \ bh \times H$$
$$= 0.5 \times 2.1 \times 17.24 \times 9.5$$
$$= 171.99 \text{ m}^3$$

$$V = A \times H$$
$$= 1/2h(a+b) \times H$$
$$= 0.5 \times 0.4(17.24+21.3) \times 9.5$$
$$= 73.23 \text{ m}^3$$

Total Volume in store
$$V = 171.99 + 73.23$$
$$= 245.22 \text{ m}^3$$

Maximum Possible Qty in Store
Mass = Density x Volume
$$= 790 Kg/m^3 \times 245.22 m^3$$
$$= 193.723 \text{ MT}$$

Maximum Possible Affected Qty
Mass = Density x Volume
$$= 790 Kg/m^3 \times 73.2 m^3$$
$$= 57.85 \text{ MT}$$

Example 37:

The policyholder reported heavy rains that accessed their warehouse through a roof section that was blown off thus causing floods therein and affecting various stacks of cereals. During the attendance, the surveyor noted that the first layer of bags on pallets was affected by the floods which attained an average height of 4 inches. The average height of pallets was 3 in. Find the maximum quantity of affected bags and their value.

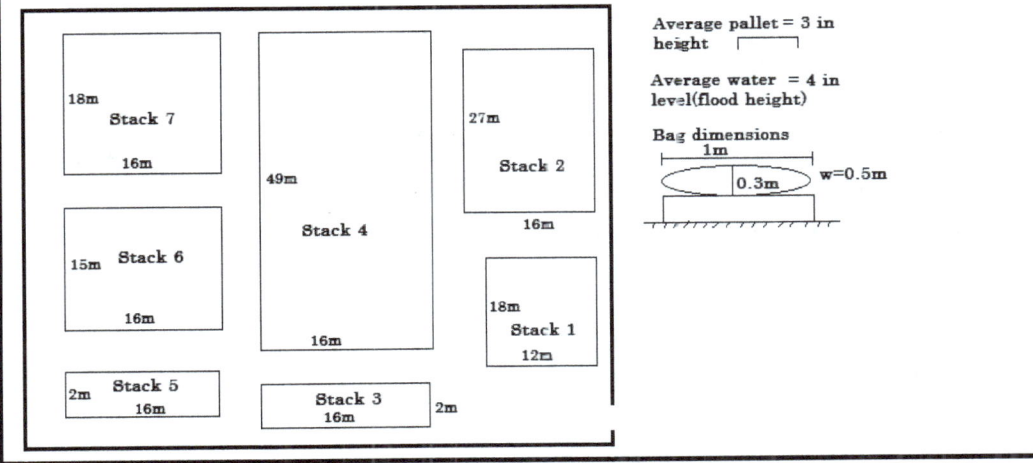

Average pallet = 3 in
height

Average water = 4 in
level(flood height)

Bag dimensions
1m

w=0.5m
0.3m

Area covered by each bag = 1m x 0.5m
$$= 0.5\text{m}^2$$

Maximum possible number of affected bags on pallets

Stack 1

GA = 16m x 18m = 288m^2

Bags on pallets = $\frac{288}{0.5}$

= 576 bags

Stack 2

GA = 16m x 27m = 432m^2

Bags on pallets = $\frac{432}{0.5}$

= 864 bags

Stack 4

GA = 16m x 49m = 784m^2

Bags on pallets = $\frac{784}{0.5}$

= 1,568 bags

Stack 3

GA = 2m x 16m = 32m^2

Bags on pallets = $\frac{32}{0.5}$

= 64 bags

Stack 5

Bags on pallets = 64 bags

Stack 6

GA = 15m x 16m = 240m^2

Bags on pallets = $\frac{240}{0.5}$

= 480 bags

Stack 7

GA = 16m x 18m = 288m^2

Bags on pallets = $\frac{288}{0.5}$

= 576 bags

Maximum number of affected bags = 576 + 864 +1568 + 64 + 64 +480 +576
= 4,192 bags

Weight of each = 50 Kg
bag

Maximum Possible Affected Qty

Total weight of = 50 Kg x 4,192
affected bags
= 209, 600 Kg
= 209.6 MT

Unit cost of each
bag from purchase = USD 1.2 per Kg
documents

Total cost of = 1.2 x 209,600 Kg
affected stock
= USD 251,520

Sum insured & value at risk

The sum insured is usually on replacement basis and is usually based on the declared values by the Insured. At the time of loss, the value at risk may be attained by acquiring the relevant stock documents including stock movement, purchase and selling costs, valuation documents and or adoption of the above methods. These are used to obtain the stock value at the time of loss. If the value at risk is greater than the sum insured and the 85% average and or appraisement clause are not applicable, then average clause shall apply.

Example 38:

Sum insured   = USD 2,000,000
Value at risk   = USD 3,600,000
Claim amount   = USD 47,000
Assessed amount = USD 30,000

Average   clause = (Sum insured/Value at risk) x Assessed amount
= (2,000,000 / 3,600,000) x 30,000
After average   = USD 16,666.67 (subject to policy terms & conditions)

7.0 BUILDINGS, STRUCTURES, FIXTURES & FITTINGS

Valuation of buildings for banking purposes is quite different from valuation for insurance purposes. Most bank valuation reports state a much lower insurance value which does not in any way represent the actual reinstatement value of the property under review. In this case, reinstatement means the cost of re-constructing the entire building from scratch (including foundation) and installing all it required fixtures & fittings in case of a total loss by a covered peril. If the policy is not on replacement or reinstatement basis, the replacement value is subjected to an appropriate depreciation to account for the period in use before the loss and n order to attain the Value at Risk. If the policy is on replacement basis, the most authoritative approach of determining its value at risk would the project value at which the contractors undertook its construction works. However, if these documents cannot be traced, a valuer can be assigned to advise on the current reconstruction cost using the similar or not significantly better construction technology. Some bank valuers understand the insurance principles and their reports can also form a basis of the sum insured or value at risk. If the structures or buildings under review are not complex (e.g. sky scrapers and the like), the valuer can follow the guide below.

7.1 Procedure for attaining the replacement and depreciated value

- Physical inspection of the property and measurement of the areas and size of the buildings especially plinth areas. If the structure has existed for some time, some software applications like google earth among others can be used to note the building areas or shapes especially in situations where the plans or layouts are not provided. During the inspection, physical defects such as wall cracks are noted and may contribute to the building life and applicable depreciation rate.

- Estimate of the reinstatement or replacement cost of the buildings /structures. If the policy is on replacement basis, the value of re-constructing the building or structures is estimated using appropriate valuation methods like the cost and comparison approach which are discussed in the following sections.

- Estimate of the indemnity or depreciated value. This includes a consideration for age of the structure and noted physical defects, useful life which form the basis of applying an appropriate depreciation rate to arrive at the depreciated value.

7.2 Comparative approach for buildings

This is the most widely used method of valuation which uses a direct comparison with prices paid for similar properties to the one being valued. The following should be noted or considered when using this approach:

- o Properties compared must be similar; e.g. four-bedroomed detached houses
- o Properties must be in the same area
- o The legal status should be the same; i.e. freehold or leasehold
- o The property transactions must be recent
- o The market must be stable
- o Rarely are two properties exactly the same and people's opinions about property are very subjective.

7.3 Contractors/ Cost approach

This is also known as the cost approach. It involves calculating the cost of rebuilding the property, as if new, including fees, etc. and applying the relevant depreciation.[6] The main concern is the amount or cost of reinstating or reconstruction of the structures or buildings in case of a total loss. It estimates the cost of building a similar structure from scratch. The value of land is not considered when valuing for insurance purposes.

Formula

Building Value = Replacement/Reproduction Cost – Depreciation

---

Example 39:

An R.C.C Roofed Residential Building of Ground Floor 1600 Sqm & First Floor 1000 sqm. Age of Ground Floor is 10 years and that of First Floor is 5 years. Find the market value of the building.

Solution

Ground floor
Plinth area of Ground floor = 1600 Sqm

Replacement Rate of construction = USD. 500 / Sqm
Replacement value = USD. 8,00,000/-
Age of the Building = 10 years
Total lift assumed = 80 years

Depreciation percentage assuming the salvage value as 10% = $\frac{10}{80}$ X 90 = 11%
Depreciation value = USD. 88,000
Depreciated value of Ground Flcor = USD. 7,12,000

First floor
Plinth area of Ground floor = 1000 Sqm
Replacement Rate of construction = USD. 400 / Sqm
Replacement value = USD. 4,00,C00
Depreciation % age (GF Dep) = 11%
Depreciation value 11/100 x 4,00.000 = USD. 44,000
Depreciated value of First Floor = USD. 3,56,000

Total value of GF & FF (7,12,000 + 3,56,000) = 10,68,000

7.4 Cost Approximating Technics

There are a number of cost approximating approaches or technics that assist in estimating the cost of a builcing and these include the interpolation method, unit method, cube method and superficia method among others.

7.4.1 Interpolation method

Interpolation is a technique used in the early stages of the design sequence when information, drawn or otherwise, on the proposed project is in short supply. It requires a good deal of skill and experience and is the process of adding in or deducting from the cost analysis figure to arrive at a budget for a new project. Therefore, in preparing a budget for a new project assume, a cost analysis has been chosen as the basis for the estimate. However, the cost analysis will contain items that are not required for the new project and these must be deducted.

For example, in the subject project may exclude certain aspects like the installation of air conditioning systems and this will have to be deducted from the budget or computation. On the other hand, the subject project may include CCTV throughout and the cost of providing this must be calculated and added in. It is important, as descrbed later, to adjust costs to take account of differences in price levels. The process continues until all identified differences have been accounted for.[6]

7.4.2 Unit method

The unit method is a single price rate method based upon the cost per functional unit of the building, a functional unit being, for example, a hotel bedroom. This method is often regarded as a way of making a comparison between buildings in order to satisfy the design team that the costs are reasonable in relation to other buildings of a similar nature.[6]

The unit method is the simplest and quickest method of estimating the cost of a proposed construction project. In this method, the surveyor counts the number of units which are going to be accommodated in a building, for example the number of occupants or main furniture objects used by an individual. The number is then multiplied by the cost per unit to get the total estimated cost of the project.[31]

Formula

Number of Units x Cost per Unit = Total Estimated Cost of Building Project.

Example 40:   In a school building, the unit is the classroom. Then, the approximate cost of the structure = Number of classrooms in the structure x cost of each classroom in the similar existing structure.

Example 41:
 	
 Given that the current cost for a 120-student school structure is USD1,200,000. Find the estimate for a 90-student school.[33]
 	
 Solution
 	
 Cost per student = USD1,200,000/120
             = USD10,000/student
 For a 90-student school = USD 10,000 X 90
                = USD 900,000

Example 42:   Given that the current cost for a 100-bed hospital constructed is USD 1,250,000. Find the estimate for a 125-bed hospital.[33]

Solution

Cost per bed = USD 1,250,000/100
             = USD12,500/bec
For a 125-bed hospital = USD12,500/bed X 125 bed
                       = USD1.562,500

Example 43:

Given that the current cost of a multistory garage spaced for 500 cars the construction cost is USD 3,000,000. Find the estimate of 450 car garage.[33]

Solution

Cost per car = USD 3,000,000/500
             = USD 6,000/car
For a 450-car garage = USD 6.000/car X 450 car
                     = USD 2,270,000

Note:

o In some cases, this rough approximation method may have a huge margin of error and the surveyor has to account for this margin by giving a cost range rather than a specific figure. An experienced consultant who has done a number of different building estimation assignments will be in a better position to give a cost guide of the proposed project. Nevertheless, the consulting surveyor can also refer to annual building cost data compiled by municipalities and property developers.[31]

o The service units for various structures are given in the below table.[32]

No.	Types of Construction	Service unit
1.	School, Collage	Classroom
2.	Hospitals	Bed
3.	Hostel	Students
4.	Hotel	Room
5.	Theatre (Cinema)	Seat
6.	Stadium	Seat
7	Stable	Animal
8	Water Tank	Liter
9	Dam	Hectare Meter
10.	Water Supply Scheme	Person
11.	Road	Kilometer
12.	Canal	Kilometer
13.	Bridge	Meter
14.	Power Station	Kilowatt

7.4.3 Cube method

This method is specific for building projects and aims to overcome the current criticism to the floor area method that does not consider possible variations of the storey height.[35] In this method, the approximate cost of the per volume (cube) is calculated from historical data and multiplied by the volume of proposed building to work out the construction cost of proposed building.[34] However, it is rarely used in practice.

In order to use this method, the building volume must be first assessed and explicit rules exist in some countries for that purpose. Buildings with distinct types of occupation should have corresponding volumes assessed separately, for example, car park areas, shopping areas and office areas in a commercial building. Specific works like excavations, foundations and external works ought to be assessed separately by using cost comparisons or approximate quantities, for example. Costs per cubic meter may be difficult to find in countries where the method is not current. Actually, such costs depend on a number of variables, like building types, proportion of wall area per floor area, quality of finishes and so on.[35]

Note:

✓ Calculation of volume is subject to rules of measurement:
   1. Measured from external faces of external walls
   2. Height of the building is taken from the top of foundation to:
      a. For pitched roof:
         - A point midway between the ceiling and the apex of roof 2/3 where roof space is un-occupied.
         - A point three quarters from the ceiling to the apex of the roof where roof space is occupied
      b. For Flat roof
         - A point 0.61m (2ft) above the roof structure

✓ All projections such as porches, steps, bays, dormers, projecting roof lights, chimney stacks, tank compartments on flat roof and similar features, shall be measured and added to the cubic content of the main building. The volume of the building so obtained is then multiplied with the unit rate to obtain the cost estimate.

7.4.4 Superficial method

The superficial method is a single price rate method based on the cost per square meter of the building. This cost can be derived from known construction rates of similar structures that have almost similar features. The use of this method should be restricted to the early stages of the design sequence and is probably the most frequently used method of approximate estimating. Its major advantage is that most published cost data is expressed in this form. The method is quick and simple to use though, as in the case of the unit method, it is imperative to use data from similarly designed projects.

Another advantage of the superficial method is that the unit of measurement is meaningful to both the client and the design team. Although the area for this method is relatively easy to calculate, it does require skill in assessing the price rate. The rules for calculating the area are:

- All measurements are taken from the internal face of external walls. No deduction is made for internal walls, lift shafts, stairwells, etc. – gross internal floor area
- Where different parts of the building vary in function, then the areas are calculated separately
- External works and non-standard items such as piling are calculated separately and then added into the estimate. Figures for specialist works may be available from sub-contractors and specialist contractors.[6]

Example 44:

Below is a plan for a 3 storey building with a basement.

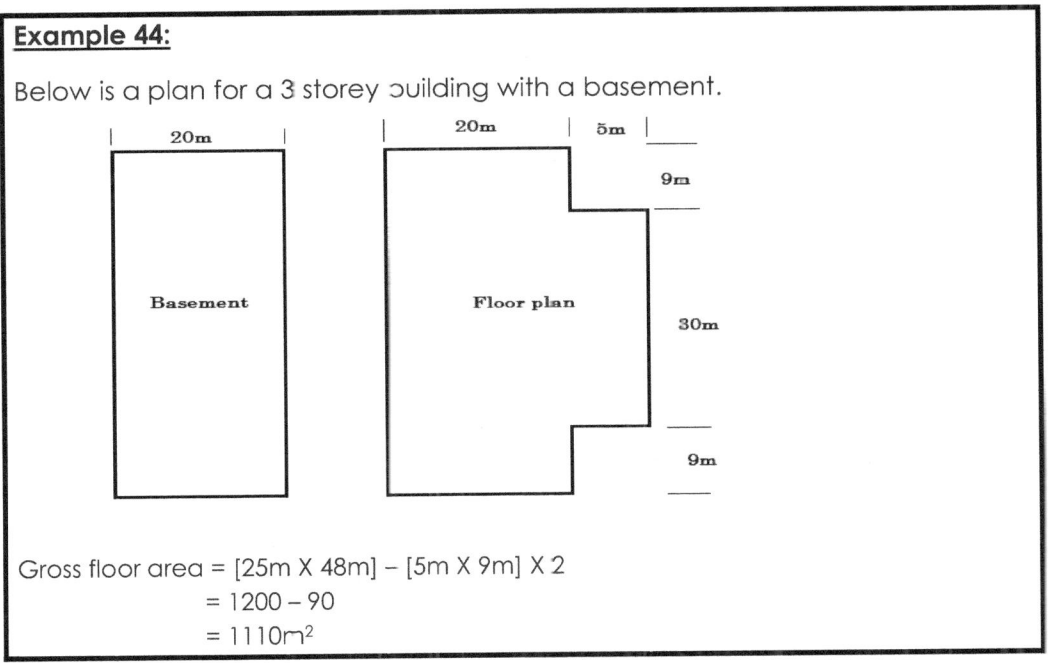

Gross floor area = [25m X 48m] – [5m X 9m] X 2

$$= 1200 - 90$$

$$= 1110m^2$$

Area of 3 floors = 1110 X 3 = 3330m²
Construction rate = USD 1500/m²
Estimate for the 3 floors = USD 1500/m² X 3330m² = USD 4,995,000
Basement area = 20 X 48 =960m²
Construction rate = USD 1800/m²
Estimate for basement = USD 1800/m² X 960m² = USD 1,728,000
Total Estimate for the building = USD 6,723,000

Note: How to derive the construction rate

✓ **Definition:** The construction rate is the cost of money charged by a builder or contractor for 1 sqm or 1sqft construction in a given area. Construction rates per sqm vary from one area to another depending on the availability of local construction material. For example, in an urban area, construction materials maybe easily available at a competitive rate, thus making the construction rate lower. In rural areas most construction material and or professional labour may not be easily available and there may arise a need to transport (or house) professional labour and construction materials thus making the construction rate higher.

Formula

Total cost of construction = Area of plot/ built-up area x Construction rate

Construction rate = Total cost of construction
                    Area of plot/ built up area

✓ **Methods 1:** This is a simple approach to a suitable construction rate. It starts with identifying a building with a known project value, construction features and technology.

For example: a 7th floor commercial building has a project value of USD 5,000,000 and built-up area of 320 sqm. The construction rate per sqm from this building would be attained by dividing the project value by the number of floors and built-up area i.e. [USD 5,000,000 / (7 x 320)] = USD 22,321 per sqm

This construction rate could be applicable to another building with approximately similar features and location among other factors.

✓ **Method 2:** This involves the computation of the relevant material and labour costs to attain the total cost of construction. This is then divided by the area covered by the building or plot to obtain the construction rate as shown below;

Example 45:

Assumptions: Standard brick size without mortar = 215 × 102.5 × 65 mm thick. Standard brick size with mortar = 225 × 112.5 × 75 mm thick. (with plaster). Standard block work size without mortar = 440 x 215 x 100 mm thick. Standard block work size with mortar = 450 x 225 x 100 mm thick (without plaster).

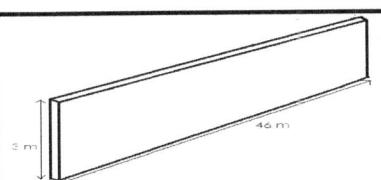

You have been assigned to advise insurance on the reinstatement value of the client's boundary wall which is composed of standard clay bricks, mortar and a plastered finishing. The wall is 3m high, 46 m long and 235mm thick. Find the replacement value of the boundary wall.

Solution.

Brick work
Assuming a header style of construction.
Area of one brick face = (112.5 x 75) x 10^{-6} m² = 8.44 x 10^{-3} m².
Bricks per m² = 119 bricks
Area of boundary wall = 3 x 46 m² = 138 m²
No. of required bricks = 16,422
Cost per brick = USD 0.1
Cost of 16,422 bricks = 0.1 x 16,422 = USD 1642.2

Mortar
Mortar ratio = 1:4
Volume of mortar = Volume of wall – volume of bricks
= (3 x 46 x 0.235) – (0.215 x 0.105 x 0.065) x 16,422
= 32.43 – 24.09 = 8.34 m³
Qty of cement = 8.34 x (1/5) = 1.668 m³ (2,401.92 Kg) (1m³ = 1,440 Kg)
One cement bag = 50 Kg (USD 9)
2,401.92 Kg = USD 432.35
Qty of Coarse sand = 8.34 x (4/5) = 6.672 m³
1 Elf truck carries 3 m³ of Sand and it cost USD 54.05
6.672 m³ = USD 120.1

Plaster
Total plaster volume = 2(3x46x0.01) + 2(3x0.235x0.01) +(46x0.235x0.01) = 3.01m³
Qty of cement = 0.602 m³ = 866.62 Kg = USD156
Qty of coarse sand = 2.408 m³ = USD 43.38

Substructure
Excavations and foundation (46x 0.5) m =USD 500

Labour
5 workers @ USD 10 per day for 30 days (5x10x30) = USD 1500
Overall total = USD 4237.93
Add profit and overheads (15%) = 4237.93x15% = USD 635.69
Total cost of construction = USD 4873.62

Construction rate = USD 4873.62/138 m² = USD 35.32/m²

Example 46:

Below is an estimate for the brick and masonry required for the construction of a room or warehouse assuming no plastering or painting is to be done.

Mortar Quantity
Volume of 1 brick	=	0.19x0.09x0.09
	=	0.001539m³
Volume of Brick with mortar	=	0.2x0.1x0.1
	=	0.002m³

Volume of Mortar for 1 brick
= Vol of Brick with mortar – Vol of 1 brick

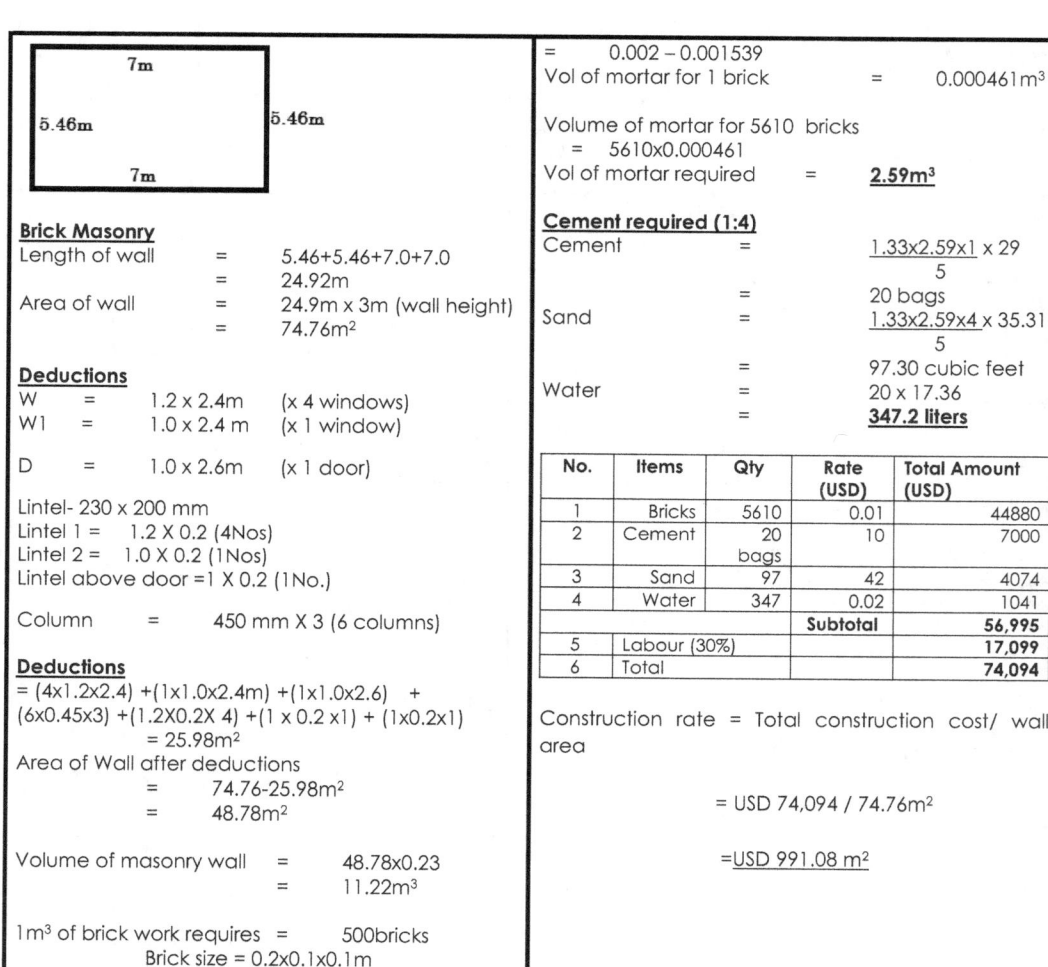

Brick Masonry

Length of wall	=	5.46+5.46+7.0+7.0
	=	24.92m
Area of wall	=	24.9m x 3m (wall height)
	=	74.76m²

Deductions

W	=	1.2 x 2.4m	(x 4 windows)
W1	=	1.0 x 2.4 m	(x 1 window)
D	=	1.0 x 2.6m	(x 1 door)

Lintel- 230 x 200 mm
Lintel 1 =   1.2 X 0.2 (4Nos)
Lintel 2 =   1.0 X 0.2 (1Nos)
Lintel above door =1 X 0.2 (1No.)

Column   =   450 mm X 3 (6 columns)

Deductions
= (4x1.2x2.4) +(1x1.0x2.4m) +(1x1.0x2.6) +
(6x0.45x3) +(1.2X0.2X 4) +(1 x 0.2 x1) + (1x0.2x1)
= 25.98m²
Area of Wall after deductions
=   74.76-25.98m²
=   48.78m²

Volume of masonry wall = 48.78x0.23
= 11.22m³

1m³ of brick work requires =   500bricks
Brick size = 0.2x0.1x0.1m
No of bricks required = 11.22 x 500
=   5610

= 0.002 – 0.001539
Vol of mortar for 1 brick   =   0.000461m³

Volume of mortar for 5610 bricks
=   5610x0.000461
Vol of mortar required   =   **2.59m³**

Cement required (1:4)

Cement	=	$\frac{1.33 \times 2.59 \times 1}{5}$ x 29
	=	20 bags
Sand	=	$\frac{1.33 \times 2.59 \times 4}{5}$ x 35.31
	=	97.30 cubic feet
Water	=	20 x 17.36
	=	**347.2 liters**

No.	Items	Qty	Rate (USD)	Total Amount (USD)
1	Bricks	5610	0.01	44880
2	Cement	20 bags	10	7000
3	Sand	97	42	4074
4	Water	347	0.02	1041
			Subtotal	56,995
5	Labour (30%)			17,099
6	Total			74,094

Construction rate = Total construction cost/ wall area

= USD 74,094 / 74.76m²

=USD 991.08 m²

7.4.5 Thumb Rule method

The thumb rule approach provides a quick estimation technique for the surveyor. It provides the general cost of reconstructing the entire building structure from scratch in case of a worst-case scenario. The computed quantities have to be related to the prevailing market prices of construction materials.

1) Thumb rule for volume of concrete required.
  ✓ For 1 ft^2 = 0.038 m^3

Example 47:

A plot has an area of 40 ft x 20 ft. Calculate the volume of concrete required for construction of a bungalow that fits in the plot.

Solution
Plot area = 40 x 20 = 800 ft^2
For 1 ft^2 = 0.038 m^3
Volume of concrete = 800 x 0.038 m^3
$\qquad\qquad\qquad$ = <u>30.4 m3</u>

---

2) Thumb rule for steel quantity required for slab, beam, footing and column for a floor.
  ✓ Residential buildings: 4.5 Kg to 4.75 Kg per ft^2 steel is required
  ✓ Commercial buildings: 5 Kg to 5.5 Kg per ft^2 steel is required

For more accurate steel Quantities (As per B N Dutta)

  o Slab = 1% of total volume
  o Beam = 2% of total volume
  o Column = 2.5% of total volume
  o Footing = 0.8% of total volume

Example 48:	**Example 49:**
A slab has dimensions of 5m x 4m x 0.15m. Calculate the amount of steel required for the slab construction.	A slab has an area of 2000 ft^2 and thickness of 0.5 ft. How much steel is required in RCC roof slab?
	✓ Thumb rule for slab minimum steel
Solution	consumption = 70 Kg/ m^3
Volume of slab = 5 x 4 x 0.15 = 3 m^3	
Amount of steel required = Volume of	Solution
concrete x Density of steel x 1%	Volume of slab = 2000 x 0.5 = 1000 ft^3
$\qquad\qquad\qquad$ = 3 x 7350 x 1%	1000 ft^3 to m^3 = 1000/35.28 = 28.35 m^3
$\qquad\qquad\qquad$ = <u>235 Kg</u>	Minimum steel required $\quad$ = 70 x 28.35
	$\qquad\qquad\qquad\qquad$ = <u>1986 Kg</u>
	$\qquad\qquad\qquad$ = Approximately 2 MT

3) Thumb rule for shuttering quantity calculation
- ✓ Shuttering cost is 15% - 18% of the total construction cost.
- ✓ Shuttering required = 6 x Qty of concrete.
- ✓ No. of ply sheets = 0.22 x Area of shuttering
- ✓ Batten Qty =19.82 x No. of ply sheets (it gives batten in RM)
- ✓ Nails = 75gms of nails per m^2 of shuttering
- ✓ Binding wire = 75gms of binding wire per m^2
- ✓ Shuttering oil (liters)= 0.065 x total shuttering area

Example 50:	Example 51:
A plywood has dimensions of 2.44m x 1.22m x 0.012m. Calculate the amount of shuttering ply required.	If a construction items needs 25 ply sheets. Calculate the batten quantity required.
Solution	Solution
Volume of slab = 2.44 x 1.22 = 2.99 m^3	Batten Qty =19.82 x No. of ply sheets
Approximately 3 m^3	Batten required = 19.82 x 25
Shuttering ply required = 0.22 x 3	= 495.5 batten
= 0.66 m^2	

7.4.6 Lump Sum Estimate

This helps to estimate to total reinstatement cost for the entire building or facility and includes some of the aspects which the valuer may not have considered in the above computations. This includes a consideration of the substructure works, finishes, fittings and services (utilities) among others. Below is an illustration showing some of the stages of reinstating a damaged structure that are usually not considered when computing the sums insured yet they are usually claimed by most policyholders after damage.

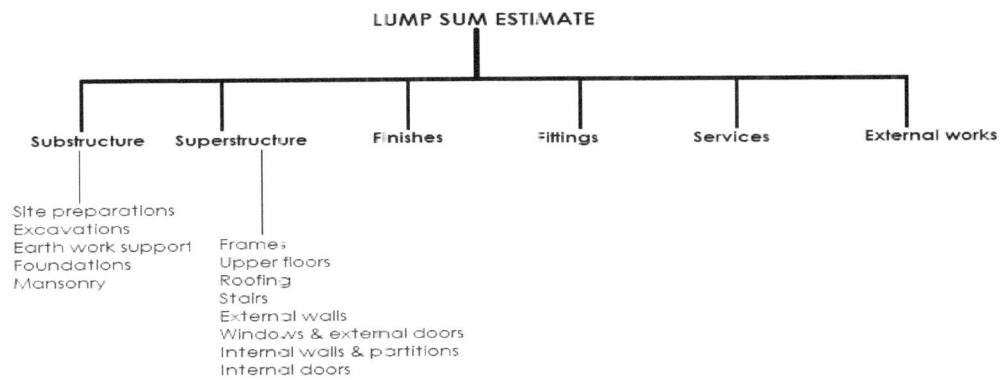

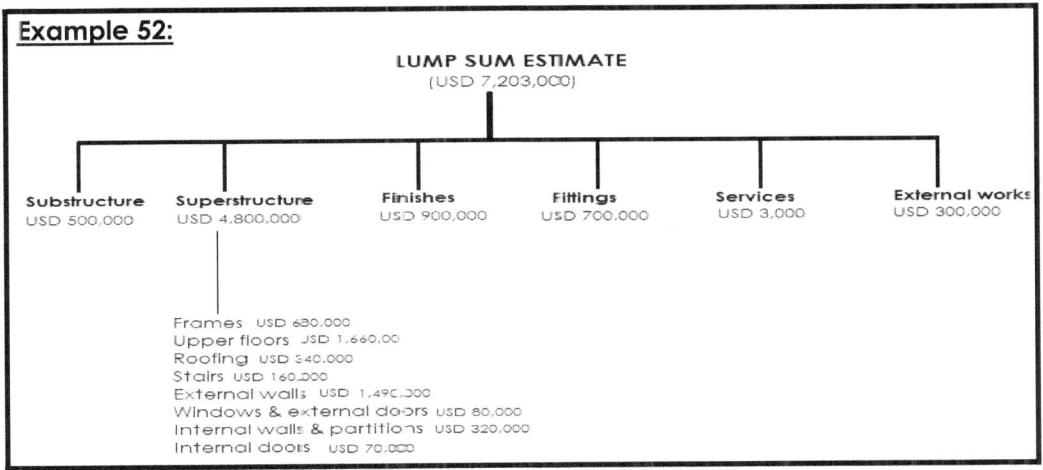

Sample estimates

a. There quite a number of sources were this estimate data can be picked like the Building Cost Information Service (BCIS) which provides cost and price data for the UK construction industry. Each country may have its own cost estimation data which may be used to estimate the reinstatement cost of buildings. For example, the latest BCIS study provides a very useful tool for benchmarking estimates or actual costs of new buildings. The table below shows the average cost per sqm for offices for each of the group elements and the total building cost. The study and or percentages also cover over 100 building types in the sectors of industrial, commercial, health, recreation, education and residential. 36

No.	Group element	Mean cost per sqm (£/m²)	Percentage (%)
1	Substructure	71	8%

2	Superstructure	394	47%
3	Internal finishes	93	11%
4	Fittings	14	2%
5	Services	264	32%
	Total	**836**	**100%**

b. According to the "Development of the Cost Baseline for Achieving Excellence in Rural Transit Facilities" in the USA, If the project is a combination of four types of facilities (administration, operation, maintenance, and vehicle storage), the cost breakdown percentages for each construction system is as tabulated below. [37]

No.	Group element	Percentage (%)
1	Demolition	1%
2	Building site work	20%
3	Substructure	13%
4	Superstructure /shell	29%
5	Internal finishes	13%
6	Services	18%
7	Equipment	6%
	Total	**100%**

c. More advanced structured may require more costs due to the need for more site work like more site mechanical and electrical utilities e.g. water supply, fuel distribution, electrical distribution and site lighting. Similarly, the interior works increase due to the need for more floors, and ceiling finishes, interior doors, partitions or walls, and fittings. The superstructure or shell and utility services also increase due to the need for more heating, ventilation, and air conditioning, plumbing, and electrical works or equipment. In this case, the cost estimate or breakdown percentages for each construction system is as tabulated below. [37]

No.	Group element	Percentage (%)
1	Demolition	0.5 %
2	Building site work	14%
3	Substructure	12%
4	Superstructure /shell	35%
5	Internal finishes	10%
6	Services	27%
7	Equipment	2%
	Total	**100%**

Example 53:

With a budget of £ 1,500,000 for constructing a single storey primary school. The overall budget was divided into reasonable percentages based on the data base of past primary schools and these percentages were allocated to each group element as tabulated below. [38]

No.	Group element	Percentage (%)	Amount (£)
1	Preliminaries	12%	120,000
2	Substructure	8%	375,000
3	Superstructure	25%	180,000
4	Finishes	12%	75,000
5	Fittings	5%	225,000
	Services	15%	225,000
	External works	15%	180,000
	Contingencies	8%	120,000
	Total	**100%**	**1,500,000**

Note:

✓ Quite often valuers or surveyors confuse fixtures and fittings while trying to separate them. Examples of fixtures include plumbing systems, tiles, doors and windows among others. These are simply defined as items that cannot be shifted after sell of a building or when shifting from a rented property.

✓ On the other hand, examples of fittings include portrait or fire extinguishers screwed on the wall, curtain blinds other items that one can possibly shift with when leaving a premise or an apartment. These may have been fitted by the tenant to contribute to the aesthetics of the room.

Sum insured & value at risk

The sum insured is usually on replacement and indemnity basis and is usually based on the declared values by the insured. At the time of loss, the value at risk may be attained by acquiring the relevant property valuation report and or adoption of the above methods. These are used to obtain the property value at the time of loss. If the value at risk is greater than the sum insured and the 85% average and or appraisement clause are not applicable, then average clause shall apply.

Example 54:

Sum insured = USD 2,000,000
Value at risk = USD 4,000,000

Claim amount	= USD 60,000
Assessed amount	= USD 35,000
Average clause	= (Sum insured/Value at risk) x Assessed amount
	= (2,000,000 / 4,000,000) x 35,000
After average	= USD 17,500 (subject to policy terms & conditions)

8.0 PLANT, MACHINERY & EQUIPMENT

The term "plant" refers to any type of machinery, equipment and apparatus used for industrial activities or processes. Generally, "machinery" are those electrical and mechanical equipment that contribute to industrial processes. Plant & Machinery represent electrical and mechanical equipment including boilers, pressure vessels, pipe systems, pipelines, telecommunication towers, silos, hoppers, metal or steel structures that may be fixed to each other and or to the earth by foundation or structural support that are used for industrial processes or activities but exclude land, buildings or any other civil structures.

8.1 Procedure for attaining the replacement and depreciated value

a. During a site inspection, the valuer is required to acquire information about the general machine operations or function and this helps in benchmarking against similar machines from historical records or potential suppliers.

b. Machinery details and specification are acquired from their panel, name plates for details like machine name, manufacturer, date of manufacture, country of origin, rating. If this information is no longer present on the machine, the valuer can seek the assistance of the section supervisors or managers in gathering data about a particular machine. This can include its technical name, manufacturer or supplier.

c. The valuer may also acquire information relating to the year of installation or commissioning, rate of use and maintenance. The machine or plant physical defects are noted and these include funny noises, worn parts and dents, rusting, faulty parts or components etc.

d. The information gathered should be related to similar machines that have ever been valued or similar machines sold by various dealers. For unique machines, the client may be required to provide a copy of their purchase invoice. After establishing the replacement value which includes the freight charges, tax charges, transport to the factory, piping, installation and commissioning charges, the valuer can apply an appropriate depreciation rate to arrive at the market value or depreciated value or value at risk.

Note:

✓ The pant & machinery depreciation rate depends on the following factors;

- Age of machine, - Condition of machine components, - Working condition - Utilization or rate of use - Machine maintenance - Working environment, - Future, economic life, Useful life - Technological and functional obsolesce, - Deterioration cue to environment condition,	- New replacement Cost - Cost of Repairs/reconditioning - Up gradation, - Impairment of functional capacity - Equioment efficiency - Scrap value - Power consumption - Raw material /spare availability - Operator skills - Price index - Acquisition cost, [27]

8.2 Comparison approach for plant & machinery

Just liked the other sections, the comparison approach is also applied here by using the acquired specifications to compare with previously valued (similar) items. Alternatively, inquiries can be conducted from the various machine suppliers or dealers for purposes of acquiring their latest replacement costs. The costs of freight, taxes, piping, installation, commissioning and, inclucing expenses for outsourced labour together with other incidental costs that apply may also be considered.

Example 55:

Peter was assigned to value various plant and machinery which also included a transformer. He acquired the necessary transformer specs or information as follows;

- Survey date: 23/04/2018 - Serial No. 194107_36 - Rated Power. 1000 KVA - Production Date (Y.O.M). 03/2012 - Manufacturer: Danish Transformer Pvt Ltd - Country of Origin: India - Date of installation: 23/04/2012 - Testing & Installation cost then: USD 500 - Testing & Installation cost now: USD 900	- Physical defects: faint color, rust, faulty breather. (Worth – USD 250) - Transformer price then: USD 22,000 - Transformer price now: USD 27,000 - Cost of freight then: USD 1,100 - Cost of freight now: USD 1,800 - Taxes then: USD 200 - Taxes now: USD 350 - Estimated useful life span: 25 years - Residual value: USD 0

Replacement Value = USD 27,000 + USD 1,800 + USD 350 + USD 900
$$= \underline{USD\ 30,050}$$

Depreciation rate = (1/25) X 100% = 4% per annum
Total dep (for 6 yrs.) = 6 X 4% = 24% (straight-line method)
$$= 24\% \ X \ USD\ 30,050$$
$$= USD\ 7,212$$

Indemnity Value = USD 30,050 – USD 7,212 – USD 250
$$= \underline{USD\ 22,588}$$

Example 56:

Tom was assigned to conduct a valuation of various plant and machinery belonging to a tea factory with a view of advising on their replacement and actual cash values. After noting down the various machine specifications and making the necessary inquiries from their dealers or manufactures, the valuation tabulated below was generated;

No	Items	Description	Qty	unit cost (USD) FOB India	Total cost (USD)	CIF Kampala (15%)	Testing, piping & Installation (5%)	Total Replacement Value (USD)	Estimated Installation Dates	useful life (years)	Depreciation rate per year	Total dep considering useful lifespan	Remaining dep /Residual value	Depreciated Value (USD)
1	Withering troughs & axial flow fans	Steels worth fans-concrete trough	16			204,100	10,205	214,305	1,989	15.5	6%	100%	30%	64,292

2	CTC Machines	Vikram 36" 4 cuts 13" Dia	1	41,121	41,121	6,168	2,056	49,345	2,018	15.5	6%	100%	30%	14,803
3	Electric panel board - ctc	Steels Worth	1	4,370	4,370	656	219	5,244	1,989	8.0	13%	100%	30%	1,573
4	Electrical panel- Vikram CTC & RV	Vikram Line	1	3,000	3,000	450	150	3,600	1,989	8.0	13%	100%	30%	1,080
5	Continuous fermenting machine	Vikram 3 + 3 modules, 8" wide, With Control Panel	2	37,265	74,530	11,180	3,727	89,436	2,018	15.5	6%	13%	87%	77,896
6	Continuous fermenting machine	Marshall Fowler	1	44,314	44,314	6,647	2,216	53,177	1,989	15.5	6%	100%	30%	15,953
7	Vibro fluid bed drier	Kilburn 2009, 650 kgmt/hr	1	62,000	60,307	9,046	3,015	72,368	2,015	15.5	6%	32%	68%	49,024
8	Power Factor correction 600 Kvar	600 Kvar	1	3,060	3,060	459	153	3,672	2,015	15.5	6%	32%	68%	2,487
9	C.T.C Conveyer	C.T.C Conveyer	1	3,501	3,501	525	175	4,201	2,018	8.0	13%	25%	75%	3,151
10	Staunch Pressure Washer & J2GE SM355 cut off machines	Extra guns and wipes for Washer	1	2,111	2,111	317	106	2,533	2,018	12.5	8%	16%	84%	2,128
11	Induction motor 7.5W/10HP	GG Drier cyclone Fan	1	631	631	95	32	757	2,018	5.0	20%	40%	60%	454
12	CTC Machines- Line 3	Gem FORGINGS	1	60,310	60,310	9,047	3,016	72,372	2,018	15.5	6%	13%	87%	63,034
13	Gear Box worm wheel	For CTC line 3 Gem forging	1	1,426	1,426	214	71	1,711	2,018	8.0	13%	25%	75%	1,283
14	Rotorvane	Vikram 18" new	1	3,961	3,961	594	198	4,754	2,020	15.5	6%	0%	100%	4,754
15	Radiator - Withering	new	1	4,112	4,112	617	206	4,934	2,020	15.5	6%	0%	100%	4,934
16	Steam boiler	Serial No. WP - 45, feed water system,	1	150,000	150,000	22,500	7,500	180,000	2,004	25.0	4%	64%	36%	64,800
17	Generator & Electrical installations	Perkins 500 KVA	1	76,767	76,767	11,515	3,838	92,120	2,018	25.0	4%	8%	92%	84,751
18	Transformer	1000 KVA	1	18,786	18,786	2,818	939	22,543	2,018	30.0	3%	7%	93%	21,041
19	Automatic change over switch	1600 amps	1	9,647	9,647	1,447	482	11,577	2,018	15.5	6%	13%	87%	10,083
	Total						USD	888,64*						487,521

Note:

✓ There are those industrial machineries that are usually fabricated by the company staff themselves. They may at times import all the necessary materials or acquire them from the local market. The valuation for these items can be based on all the necessary costs required to put together the entire machine assembly.

8.3 Cost approach for plant & machinery

Under this method. the valuer obtains the machinery purchase documents from the client which show the exact value at which each machine was procured and installed. These may include purchase invoices, freight, clearing and tax charges, invoices or receipts for transportation, labour and installing and commissioning fees among others. This is the most authoritative way of the computing up the machine replacement value (especially for unique/industrial machinery) since t adds up all the costs that were involved in acquiring the machine and provides a replacement value that main not easily be disputed. This approach can also best apply on brand new unique equipment which may be less than 2 years old. To use this approach, the machine must have been acquired from an authoritative supplier or dealer (due to warranty issues) in a brand-new condition since some clients sell their properties under unusual circumstances, at a much lower values compared to their known market values. In this case the most authoritative value is the current market value from suppliers or dealers not the client to client purchase agreement which may also be considered as forced sales conditions where one party is in urgent need of funds.

Example 57:

Peter was assigned to value a unique machinery which was specifically designed for the client's factory. He acquired the machinery information and used it to compute its value at risk.

- Serial No. 798WT107_QPD - Invoice price (FOB): USD 22,000 - Production Date (Y.O.M). 03/2010 - Country of Origin: UK - Date of installation: 23/03/2010 - Testing & Installation cost : USD 500	- Physical defects: none worth noting - Cost of freight: USD 1,100 - Taxes then: USD 200 - Estimated useful life span: 25 years - Residual value: USD 0

Purchase Value = USD 22,000 + USD 1,100 + USD 200 + USD 500
                = USD 23,800

Depreciation rate   = (1/25) X 100%   = 4% per annum
Total dep (for 6 yrs.) = 6 X 4% = 24% (straight-line method)
                    = 24% X USD 23,800
                    = USD 5,712

Value at Risk   = USD 23,800 – USD 5,712
                    = USD 18,088

8.4 Depreciation approaches including the use-base method

Under this method, a depreciation charge is made a function of usage rather than a function of time. The basic assumption of this method is that, with every unit of product, the value of the asset reduces proportionately. So, depreciation under this method becomes a true variable cost of the product. This method is suitable where individual output can easily be identified. [11]

There are three methods based on this concept:

- ✓ Output method
- ✓ Working hours method,
- ✓ Mileage method. (explained in the next section)

8.4.1 Output method

Under this method, a depreciation charge for the year is made to vary with the number of units produced during the years. To find out depreciation, the cost less salvage value of the asset is divided by the number of units expected to be produced by the asset during its service life.

Depreciation cost per unit = $\dfrac{\text{Cost of asset - Salvage value}}{\text{Estimated number of units}}$

Periodic depreciation
= No. of units produced (during the period) x Depreciation cost per unit.

Depreciation Expense = Dep. Rate per unit × Units used.

Example 58:

A truck that was purchased for USD 30,000 with a residual value of USD 2,000 and a life of 100,000 miles. During the period between June-Sept, the truck recorded 5,200 miles of use. What is the units-of-production depreciation for the truck during the period?

Solution:
Depreciation Rate per unit = (30,000 – 2,000) / 100,000
                        = USD 0.28/mile
Depreciation   = 0.28 x 5,200
                        = USD 1,456

Example 59:

A coin machine costing USD 200,000 has a salvage value of USD 20,000 at the end of its economic life of five years. The schedule of production per year is as follows: [24]

Year	1	2	3	4	5
Number of Coins	100,000	80,000	60,000	40,000	20,000

Determine the annual reserve for depreciation for the third year only.

Solution

Total number of coins = 100,000 + 80,000 + 60,000 + 40,000 +20,000
                     = 300,000
Depreciation per unit = (C - S) / Total number of coins
                      = (200,000 - 20,000) / 300,000
                      = 0.60
Depreciation reserve for the third year.
                      = 0.60 x 60,000
                      = USD 36,000

8.4.2 Working hours method

This method is suitable where the life of asset is measured by its service hours rather than units produced. To find out depreciation, the cost of asset less salvage value is divided by the total working hours during its life.

So, Depreciation cost per hour = $\dfrac{\text{Cost of asset - Salvage value}}{\text{Total working hours of the asset}}$

Period depreciation
= Number of hours worked during the period X Depreciation cost per hour.

Example 60:

A machine costs USD 400,000 with a salvage value of USD 200,000. Its useful life is six years. In the first year, it is used for 4000 hours. In the second year, 6000 hours and 8000 hours on the third year. The expected flow of the machine is 38000 hours in six years. Compute the machine depreciation at the end of the second year [24]

Solution

Depreciation per hour = (C - S) / Total number of hours
                      = (400,000 - 20,000) / 38000
                      = USD 10

Depreciation at the end of 2nd year.
                      = 10 x 6000
                      = USD 60,000

Note:

✓ The depreciation for the plant and machinery is not limited to the above methods only but also includes the straight-line and reducing balance methods among other applicable methods.

Sum insured & value at risk

The sum insured is usually on replacement and indemnity basis and is usually based on the declared values by the insured. At the time of loss, the value at risk may be attained by acquiring the relevant machinery valuation report, asset register showing the machines and their purchase values and or adoption of the above methods. These are used to obtain the machinery values at the time of loss. If the value at risk is greater than the sum insured and the 85% average and or appraisement clause are not applicable, then average clause shall apply.

Example 61:	
Sum insured	= USD 5,000,000
Value at risk	= USD 12,000,000
Claim amount	= USD 50,000
Assessed amount	= USD 45,000
Average clause	= (Sum insured/Value at risk) x Assessed amount
	= (5,000,000 / 12,000,000) x 45,000
After average	= USD 18,750 (subject to policy terms & conditions)

9.0 MOTOR VEHICLE VALUATION

Motor valuation involves valuation of all movable machines like vehicles, trucks, forklifts, excavators, graders among other machinery with registration plates. The valuation procedure or methods used here are similar to some of those explained in the above sections.

9.1 Procedure for attaining the replacement and market value

a. During the physical inspection, the machine specifications are noted including mileage, chassis number, body description and engine number & capacity, internal and external accessories. The inspection also includes identification of relevant component defects such as dents, bends, significant scratches and unusual machine sounds which may indicate worn out, faulty parts.

b. If need be, the machine or vehicle can also be started or road tested in order properly establish its working conditions including all the relevant accessories. The general working condition of the machine or vehicle has a great effect on its lifespan and depreciation rate. Sometimes the manufacturer or brand also affected the useful life and depreciation rates as well.

c. The valuer can either acquire the relevant machine purchase documents and or make independent inquiries from various dealers /authoritative websites or publications which may guide in forming a general opinion of the current replacement value that closely matches the one under consideration. For items that have to be imported, the relevant Free on Board (FOB), freight, clearing, transportation, taxation and registration charges have to be computed or considered in in order to attain an appropriate replacement value. In most cases, bond vehicles include a profit margin rate or charge for the seller who imported them and this may be considered sometimes when determining the vehicle market value.

d. An appropriate depreciation rate is then applied basing on the general condition of the item, period in use, useful or lifespan, rate of use, environment of use, rate of maintenance, brand, noted physical defects among other factors to establish its market value or value at risk.

Note:

✓ If a test drive is not possible, the valuer can interact with the various vehicle users, drivers, operators to acquire information about the functionality of the vehicle/machine and its systems or components. Some of the information can then be sampled for its accuracy before its adopted.

9.2 Comparison method for motor vehicles & movable machines

In this method, the valuer obtains the vehicle/ machine specifications and compares them with similar vehicles on the market. The items chosen should have the closest specifications to the item under consideration.

9.3 Cost approach for motor vehicles & movable machines

Under this method, the valuer obtains the vehicle/ machine purchase documents including its purchase agreement or invoice, freight charges, transport, clearing charges, tax charges and registration fees among others. This is the most authoritative way of the computing vehicle or machine replacement value especially for unique brands or models. It also adds up all the costs that were involved in acquiring the asset and provides a replacement value that main not easily be disputed. Under unusual circumstances, some clients usually sell their vehicles at much lower values compared to their known market values. In this case the most authoritative value is the current market value from suppliers or dealers not the client to client purchase agreements.

Example 62:

A valuer was assigned to conduct a valuation of a clients' vehicle for insurance purposes. The Insurer wanted to know is current condition and market value to enable them set the right premiums. Below are some of the field notes that were taken.

Data from physical inspection and Interviews

Vehicle description		Serviceability of components	
Make	Toyota	Chassis/ Sub Frame	In good condition
Model	Landcruiser	Body Shell/Cabin/Pant	Faint
Y.O.M	2003	Interior/ Seats	Two front seats are torn
Body description	Ambulance	Engine	Has leakages
Transmission	Manual	Clutch	In good condition
Colour	White	Gear Box	In good condition
Engine	1HZ–0420245 (4164 cc)	Suspension System	In good condition
Chassis Number	JTERB71J800017643	Shock Absorbers	In good condition
Fuel	Diesel	Steering System	In good condition
Mileage	196,496 Km	Electrical System	In good condition
Country of Origin	Japan	Extras Fitted	Dead radio
Date of Reg.	12/09/2003	Tyres	Front tyres are worn out
Previous owner	None	Siren	Faulty
		Windows/ Glasses	Cracks in wind screen, broken left side mirror
		Bonnet lock handle	Missing
		Last service date	20/05/2019

Determination of the current vehicle market value

Option 1: Inquiries from local bonds for Similar vehicles

No	Description	Y.O M	Mileage	Chassis No.	Engine	Body description	Price (USD)
1	Toyota land cruiser	2007	100,346 Km	JTERB652430005	3500 cc	Ambulance	81,000
2	Toyota land cruiser	2015	62,032 Km	JTERB652430091	4500 cc	Ambulance	130,000
3	Toyota land cruiser	2001	257,940 Km	JTERBC53430046	3000cc	Ambulance	38,000

Option 2: Inquiries from local dealers or local websites

No	Description	Y.O.M	Mileage	Chassis No.	Engine	Body description	Price (USD)
1	Toyota land cruiser	2019	30,846 Km	JTELB71J907090971	4700 cc	Pickup D Cabin	230,000
2	Toyota land cruiser	2000	209,713 Km	JTERB004430091	3200 cc	Hardtop	34,000
3	Toyota land cruiser	2005	188,344 Km	JTERB053437853	4,000cc	Ambulance	56,000

Option 3: Inquiries from online dealers

No	Description	Y.O.M	Mileage	Chassis No.	Engine	Body description	Price (USD) FOB Japan
1	Toyota land cruiser	2004	180,220 Km	JTELB71J9000058	4300 cc	Ambulance	58,367
2	Toyota land cruiser	2003	170,107 Km	JTERB55479321177	3500 cc	Ambulance	43,349
3	Toyota land cruiser	2001	191,511 Km	JTER467889300368	4000 cc	Ambulance	40,378

<u>Example for option 3 (item No.1): Government policy in Uganda on imported vehicles and estimated charges</u>

No.	Item description	% charged	Amount (USD)
1	Vehicle value (FOB) – USD 23,100		
2	CIF Mombasa	15% to - 25% of FOB	28,875
3	Transport & expenses from Mombasa to Kampala	Depends on destination	487
4	Clearing agent fees	Depends	54
5	Import duty	25% of CIF Mombasa	7,219
6	VAT	18% of CIF Mombasa	5,198
7	Withholding Tax	6% of CIF Mombasa	1,733
8	Environmental Tax	50% of CIF Mombasa	14,438
9	Registration & plate expenses	1.3% of CIF Mombasa	365
	CIF Kampala/ Landed cost		**58,367**

<u>Government policy on imported vehicles, environmental tax breakdown</u>

Depends on Year of Manufacture from current date	
0 to 5yrs	NIL
0 to 10yrs	20% of CIF Mombasa
10yrs & ABOVE	50% of CIF Mombasa

Option 4: The client submits the vehicle purchase documents or agreement.

Description	Toyota land cruiser	Seller	M/s quality vehicle bond Ltd
Y.O.M	2003	Buyer	Mr. Ochan Peter
Mileage	196,496 Km	Purchase date	14/05/2018
Chassis No.	JTERB71J800017643	Purchase Amount	USD 254,000
Engine	4164 cc	Balance	Nil

<u>Note:</u>

- ✓ **Option 1 & 2** are good options for a more precise or accurate valuation since the seller/dealer can be easily reached or directly contacted. The values under these options already have the profit margin and taxation aspects. Caution should be taken when considering **option 2** due to the fact that some low-cost second-hand vehicles may have un-declared mechanical or electrical issues.

- ✓ **Option 3** can most appropriately be applied on unique vehicle brands or personal imported vehicles otherwise you may have to add a profit margin of about 10% to 30% of the landed cost if the vehicle was purchased from a dealer or bond.

- ✓ **Option 4** is the best since it cannot be disputed by the client/ vehicle owner since it's a fact from their own purchase documents. This may not apply to all vehicles that have been in use for quite some time as market forces may have changed drastically. The valuer can then apply an appropriate depreciation rate to the arrive at the current market value. In situations where this information has not been revealed, then the valuer can make use of the other options.

Example 63:

Straight line depreciation method:

Let's assume D = Annual depreciation rate, C = Estimated cost of the asset, S = Salvage/ scrap Value, V = Value after depreciation, n = Estimated Life in years depending physical inspection and inquiries.

Formula

$D = [1/n]$

Given R years, Total depreciation = R x D

Asset value after R years $V_R = [C - S] \times (1 - [R \times D])$

Question: The established replacement value of a vehicle is USD 1,000. Its estimated lifespan is 30 years. Scrap value is USD 100. Find the market value after 3 years.

Solution

Estimated life span = 30 years. Useful life span after considering the usage rate, loading rate, maintenance, noted physical defects, worn out parts etc. = 15 years

$D = [1/n] = [1/15] = 0.06667$

Given 3 years, total depreciation = 3 x 0.067 = 0.20001

Asset value after 3 years = [1000 – 100] x (1 – 0.20001)

= 900 x 0.8

Market Value   = USD 720

Example 64:

Declining balance methods:

The established replacement value of a vehicle is USD 1,000. Its estimated lifespan is 30 years. Scrap value is USD 100. Find the market value after 3 years.

Solution

Estimated life span = 30 years
Useful life span after considering the usage rate, loading rate, maintenance, noted physical defects, worn out parts etc. = 15 years
Dep. Rate, $r = 1 - [(S/C]^{1/n}$
$$= 1 - [100/1000]^{1/15} = 1 - (0.1)^{1/15}$$
$$= 0.1423$$
Value after 3 years, $V_n = C [1 - r]^n$
$$V_3 = 1000 [1 - 0.1423]^3$$
$$= 1000 \times 0.63097$$
$$= \underline{USD\ 630.97}$$
If the scrap value is zero (i.e. S = 0)
Then the dep. Rate, $r = 1/n$
$$= 1/15$$
$$= 0.06667$$
Value after 3 years, $V_n = C [1 - r]^n$
$V_3 = 1000 [1 - 0.06667]^3$
$$= 1000 \times 0.8130$$
Market Value $\qquad = \underline{USD\ 813.02}$

9.4 Mileage method

When applying this method, the working life of the vehicle or machine is expressed in mileage or kilometers. Depreciation per kilometer is calculated by dividing the cost of the vehicle by the estimated running kilometers it can travel in its life time.

So, Depreciation cost per mile / kilometer = $\dfrac{\text{Cost} - \text{Salvage value}}{\text{Estimated miles / kilometers run during the service life.}}$

Periodic depreciation
= Actual miles or km run covered during the period x Dep. cost per mile or kilometer.

Note:

- ✓ This method of depreciation accurately examines the period of use of the vehicle or machine. Its estimated useful mileage should be acquired from hand books or manuals provided by its dealers or manufacturer among other authoritative sources.

Example 65:

A truck was purchased on 1/04/ 2018 at a cost of USD 1,000,000 and it can be disposed of for USD 100,000. The expected life of truck in Kilometers will be 100,000 Km. The following table shows the total running kilometers of the truck during the particular year in the next 5 years. [25]

Date	31/03/2019	31/03/2020	31/03/2021	31/03/2022	31/03/2023
Total Kilometers covered	9,000	10,000	9,500	9,700	12,000

Calculation of amount of depreciation under Mileage or Kilometers method of Depreciation.

Solution

Amount of Depreciation per Kilometer = $\underline{\text{Cost of the asset} - \text{Salvage value of asset}}$
$$\text{Total life of the asset (in Kilometers)}$$

Depreciation (per kilometers) = 1,000,000 – 100,000 / 100,000
   = <u>USD 10 per kilometers</u>

Amount of depreciation year by year

Year	Total Kilometers covered per year	Rate of Depreciation (Per kilometer)	Amount of Depreciation for Year
2018 – 2019	9,000	10	90,000
2019 – 2020	10,000	10	1,00,000
2020 – 2021	9,500	10	95,000
2021 – 2022	9,700	10	97,000
2022 – 2023	12,000	10	1,20,000

Note: (summary for motor valuation)

- ✓ Different sellers/ dealers or agents sell at different margins. As such the same vehicle may have completely different values due to the individual business expenses and market trends among other factors.

- ✓ It is close to impossible for a valuer to find the exact similar vehicle with similar or exact specifications. In this case, a range can be adopted for a more accurate analysis.

✓ After attaining the value of a second hand or brand-new vehicle, the valuer may apply the relevant depreciation methods (depending on the available data).

✓ In the above example, the fact that the vehicle was manufactured in 2003 does not mean that it has been constantly in use since them. It may have spent some time in the bonds. Therefore, a more accurate depreciation rate can be taken from the vehicle logbook which shows the dates when it was first registered since clients are required to first register their vehicles before using them on the road. Alternatively, its purchase agreement can indicate when the client officially acquired and started using it.

✓ Other important factors to consider when valuing vehicles or mobile equipment may include its manufacturer or brand (e.g. some brands deteriorate faster), registration plate number, manufacture date, availability of spares, scarcity in the market, physical condition, defects, maintenance etc. Some of these can also contribute to an appropriate useful life which can lead to appropriate depreciation rate.

Sum insured & value at risk

In most motor policies, the basis of valuation in the vehicle market value. The sum insured is usually based on the declared values by the insured. At the time of loss, the value at risk may be attained by applying the most appropriate method above. The selected method should provide an appropriate pre-accident value of the asset which is also known as the value at risk. If the value at risk is greater than the sum insured, then average clause shall apply.

Example 66:
Sum insured   = USD 20,000
Value at risk   = USD 25,000
Claim amount   = USD 13,000
Assessed amount   = USD 8,000
Average   clause = (Sum insured/Value at risk) x Assessed amount
= (20,000 / 25,000) x 8,000
After average   = USD 6,400 (subject to policy terms & conditions)

10.0 AGRICULTURE VALUATION

Agriculture is the science or practice of farming, including cultivation of the soil for the growing of crops and rearing of animals to provide food and other products. Agriculture has always been an economic activity particularly prone to unpredictable and uncontrollable losses. From the earliest days of agriculture farmers have worried about losing production as a result of adverse natural factors.

10.1 Crop insurance

Crop insurance is a type of protection that covers agricultural producers against unexpected loss of projected crop yields or profits from produce sales. Some

78

crop insurance covers are arranged such that the insurance element is made as part of the loan, with the bank being the first recipient of any indemnity paid by the Insurer, while the premium is a working capital item that is packaged with the loan itself. In some cases, some banks may be interested in direct coverage of portions of their loan portfolios especially for catastrophic losses following a systemic peril.

Crop credit Insurance provides cover to the banks/institutions in case the farmers are not able to pay back the outstanding crop loan, which they have obtained for the purpose of sowing, cultivating and harvesting of crops, due to the natural disasters, diseases and other covered perils. Crop credit insurance is generally recommended because it automatically makes the crop loan borrower, a subscriber to the crop insurance program and ensures that the insured risks are spread widely over members. It also protects the credit system from the dynamics of changing weather on the agricultural production system. It has the following objectives:

o To provide a measure for financial support to farmers in the event as a result of covered perils.
o To restore the credit eligibility of farmers after crop failure for the next crop season.
o To support and stimulate farming and production of certain crops.

There are two major types of crop insurance covers/products namely;
a. Crop hail insurance
b. Multi-Peril Crop Insurance (MPCI)

10.1.1 Crop hail / Named peril

Crop-hail insures against crop damage caused by hail and may also include extended coverages like fire and lightning. Hail insurance has been in existence in some form since the early part of the 20th century and has been a thriving segment of the insurance industry since the 1920s. Its loss adjustment and eventual indemnity is based on a measure of the actual percentage of damage after the loss incident/event. The sum insured is agreed when the policy is purchased. Farmers who purchase crop-hail coverage can choose to drop coverage for hail under the multiple peril policy, in exchange for a reduction in premium, or keep it for additional protection. Crop-hail policies often have a low or even no deductible. Unlike other perils like drought, hail can completely destroy a portion of crops in one area of a farm but leave other crops undamaged. This type of insurance is not suitable for perils which can mpact over wide areas, e.g. drought, pest, disease. Due to its limitations, this insurance is purchased much less frequently than MPCI but can be purchased at any point in the growing season. [39]

10.1.2 Multi-peril Crop Insurance (MPCI)

Multiple peril crop insurance, protects against low yield and crop quality losses due to adverse weather (including hail, frost, wind storm, drought, excessive rainfall) and unavoidable damage from uncontrollable pests and diseases. Other covered perils may include physical loss or damage to growing crops directly by flooding, fire, lightning, malicious damage, earthquake, riot and strikes and explosion. The cover can also be extended to include harvested yield being stored at the farm or any other place of temporary storage or to apply when the crop is in transit to any recognized destination within the country.[39]

MPCI policies are meant for perils of nature whose individual contribution to a crop loss is difficult to measure. They are suited to perils which impact over a period of time. The basis for determining the percentage shortfall after a loss event can be established using the farmer's yield history, and the yield s measured at harvest. The insured yield may typically be in the range of 50 to 70 percent of historic average yield and yield shortfall may be determined on either an area or individual farmer basis.[39]

Basis for the sum insured

The valuation or computation of the sum insured is as per the input costs or expected crop yield as per the Post emergent report prepared by an agronomist. This emergence report usually provides information including the farm details, planted area, kilograms seed planted per hectare, cultivar, seed batch number, planting date, actual percentage of germination, plant density, evenness of the emerged plants, presence of deficiency symptoms, presence of plant diseases, weed control, root development, signs of wilting, growth stage and estimated yield. The client usually has the option to insure 100% of the input loan facility obtained for crop production or Production costs incurred in running the farm or business including the cost of inputs, seeds, fertilizer, ploughing, weeding, agrochemicals etc. The sum insured can as well be computed basing on the expected yield as follows;

Sum Insured = Planted Area (Acre) x Long Term Average Yield (kg/acre) x Pre-Agreed Value (USD/kg) x Guaranteed Yield.

Note:

- ✓ The guaranteed yield is a percentage of the total yield production from which claims are considered and is calculated as a percentage of the Long-Term Average Yield.
- ✓ The Long-Term Average Yield is the average yield expressed in tons per hectare achieved over the previous 5 (five) growing seasons and agreed by the Insurer on all the lands planted on the Insured's farms after receiving accurate Average Yield data/ documentation acceptable to the Insurer.
- ✓ The planted area is the productive area of each land (in acres/hectares), which should be clearly mapped and excludes headlands, access ways and contours as per crop certificate.
- ✓ The Pre-agreed value is the insured crop value per Ton (including VAT) selected by the Insured and accepted by the Insurer and would be used for the calculation of the sum insured, premiums and claims settlement. This value cannot be altered during the season.
- ✓ Expected crop yield / value for the harvested crop can also be calculated as follows i.e. = size of area planted acreage x the usual output of the farm (kgs/acre) x estimated value of harvested crop (USD per Kg).

Differences Between Crop-hail and Multiple Peril Insurance

- ▪ MPCI policies are geared to a level of expected yield, rather than the damage that is measured after a defined loss event as for the case of hail crop policies.
- ▪ An MPCI policy uses unit coverage levels rather than by acre as with crop-hail. In this case, a unit is the entire acreage of the crop planted in the county by the farmer and can be broken down into sections, square mile, or

by irrigated and dryland practices. When the loss happens under a MPCI, amount of the loss/reduced yield is averaged out over all the fields in the unit rather than over the affected acre or acres insured.

- Unlike crop-hail, a farmer cannot suddenly decide to buy a multiple peril policy. The MPCI coverage must be purchased prior to certain dates set by the state which vary according to the county and the crop. Coverage takes effect once the crop is planted but the crop must be planted before the last government established planting date for crop or county and it may not be added during the growing season.
- Crop hail coverage generally provides coverage from the first dollar of loss, although deductibles are offered, whereas multiple peril coverage includes what amounts to a deductible, guaranteeing up to 100% of expected market price but not 100% of yield.

Value at risk for Hail or MPCI

There are usually no cases were a damaged/affected crop is declared a constructive total loss or write off. In cases were the insured crop area is less than the actual area, the Insurer only compensates for losses on a pro-rata or proportionate basis. Incases were the insured crop area is more than the actual area, the Insurer only compensates for losses on the actual area. In case of insured loans, the value at risk is the outstanding loan amount at the time of loss.

Example 67: Under Insurance - Insured crop area = 150 acres - Actual area at the time of loss = 270 acres - Indemnity/proportionate loss = 150/270 = 55%
Example 68: Over Insurance - Insured crop area = 300 acres - Actual area at the time of loss = 160 acres Indemnity = Insured limit = 160 which is used for computing the loss
Example 69: Loan amount - Sum Insured/ limit as per declaration schedule/ loan amount= USD 100,000 - Claim amount = USD 90,000 - Outstanding balance at the time of loss/ Value at Risk = USD 80,000 - Assessed amount = 80,000 x percentage loss (Subject to the relevant policy provisions like excess etc.)

Indemnity computation

When indemnifying the Insured for a yield shortfall, the Loss Adjuster usually verifies the Actual Yield Harvested on all lands planted with the insured crop. If in the opinion of the Adjuster, the Potential Yield is less than the Insured Yield, then the Potential Yield is used in place of the Insured Yield in the calculation of the Guaranteed Yield. The claim would be computed as follows;

a. <u>Basing on expected yields</u>

- Sum Insured = Guaranteed Yield (ton/ha) x Pre-Agreed Market Value (USD /ton) x Insured Area (ha)
- Value Harvested = Actual Harvested Yield (ton/ha) x Insured Area (ha) x Pre-Agreed Value (USD/ton)
- Claim Payable = Sum insured – Value Harvested

b. <u>Basing on Cost of production</u>

- Sum insured = Cost of production / acre (USD) x Total acreage
- Actual percentage loss = (Guaranteed yield – Actual Yield harvested) / 100% Guaranteed Yield
- Claim payable (USD) = Actual percentage loss x Sum Insured

Note:

✓ The Actual Yield Harvested is the actual yield of crop harvested per farm plus any additional tonnage including but not limited to any grain held back for seed, feeding to livestock or any other reason and un-harvested grain.
✓ The insured yield is the long-term average yield which has already been defined in the above sections
✓ The potential yield is the harvestable yield per farmer that the crop has the potential to produce by normal growth processes had there not been a loss or losses due to a defined event covered by this Policy.

10.1.3 Crop Revenue Insurance

Under normal demand/supply conditions, a yield shortfall might be expected to result in a rise in price. To some extent such a rise will cancel out the financial loss for the grower who suffers a production shortfall. But this will only be the case if he harvests sufficient crop and sells it at sufficient price over the expected market price. This type of insurance is designed to meet any remaining shortfall in revenue from crop sales and involves the determination of loss on an area basis.

The crop revenue guarantees a certain level of revenue rather than just production and protects from declines in both crop prices and yields. The guarantee is based on market prices and the actual yield on the farm. This also leads to a consideration of farm loan and insurance linkages, since the servicing of interest and principal payments on an agricultural loan depend on the income stream produced.[39]

Computation of crop revenue insurance

Revenue Protection (RP) uses future market prices and the approved Actual Production History (APH) yields or trend-adjusted APH approved yield to compute the crop insurance revenue guarantee. It is computed by multiplying the APH approved yield or the trend-adjusted APH approved yield by the coverage level and the greater of the projected price or harvest price. The actual crop insurance revenue is computed by multiplying the actual yield by the crop insurance harvest price. The RP policy always pays a claim if the actual yield falls below the yield guarantee. The yield guarantee is computed by multiplying the APH yield for the unit, by the chosen coverage level e.g. 50% to 85%. This approach applies for a revenue protection product that includes a harvest option. On the other hand, there is an option for a RP policy with a Harvest Price Exclusion (RP-HPE) and is computed by multiplying the APH approved yield or the trend-adjusted APH yield by the coverage level and the projected price.[39]

Note:

✓ When the projected price is higher or equal to the harvest price, the revenue guarantees for RP and RP-HPE are identical.
✓ When the harvest price is greater than the projected price, the revenue guarantee for RP is higher than the revenue guarantees for RP-HPE.

Example 70:

The average December corn future price during February is USD 5.00. The APH yield is 185 bushels per acre. and the coverage level chosen is 85%. Thus, the revenue guarantee or sum insured is (USD 5.00 x 185 bsh x 85%) per acre which is

---

equal to USD 786.25 for both RP and RP-HPE.

Example 71:

The revenue guarantee is for corn and soya bean is USD 787 and USD 650 per acre. The whole farm revenue guarantee for a 50%-50% corn-soybean rotation is (USD 787 + USD 650)/2= USD 718.5

10.1.4 Index based crop Insurance

Conventional crop insurance pays individual farmers for their verified losses and evidence of damage to the actual crop on the farm or area is required before settlement. However, verifying such damage is expensive as well as the cost of making an accurate measurement of the loss on each individual farm. With an index policy, a meteorological measurement is used as the basis for indemnity payments. These damaging weather events might be a certain minimum temperature for a minimum period of time, a certain amount of rainfall in a certain time period (this can be used for excess rain and also for lack of rain or drought cover) and a certain wind speed (for hurricane insurance). Index insurance pays all insured farmers in an area the same amount based on an estimate of average losses. The differences in payouts illustrate a basis risk which is the chance that an index insurance payout will be more or less than an actual individual loss.

The index/coupon gives a monetary sum which becomes payable on approval that the named weather event of specified severity has occurred. The face value of the coupon may be triggered once the weather event has taken place for the area covered. Alternatively, it could be graduated with the value of the coupon then being proportional to the severity of the event. This basis operates over an area encompassing many insured farms and cannot be used for certain perils like hail were the adverse event normally impacts on a very limited area of land. The basic payment structure of a weather-indexed product centers around two main values i.e. the threshold and the limit. The threshold denotes the value of the index at which indemnity payments kick in while the limit denotes the point at which payments reach a maximum level. Indemnity payments typically increase as the index approaches to the limit, with the rate of increase as a function of the threshold and the actual value of the weather index.

Example 72:

Consider an index-based policy covering drought-related losses. Here the relevant weather index could be the total accumulated rainfal during a specific period of time measured in millimeters (mm). Assume a threshold of 120 mm, a limit of 60 mm, and that the policyholder buys a liability of $100,000. Since this policy provides insurance against defcit rainfall, the payment rate could be defined as the difference

Note:

- ✓ Besides high costs, agricultural index insurance overcomes two key problems with conventional insurance i.e. adverse selection and moral hazard.
- ✓ Adverse selection in agriculture is when farmers who are more likely to suffer losses are the only ones who buy insurance.
- ✓ Moral hazard mcy come in when covered farmers cut back on effort or compromise yields for the specific purpose of receiving an insurance payment.
- ✓ Index insurance overcomes both adverse selection and moral hazard because the index is based on factors that cannot be influenced by any one person.

10.2 Livestock Insurance

After crops, livestock is the second source of food as well as livelihood. In every nation, millions of households cepend on livestock as their primary or secondary source of income. This however comes with a lot of risks which include death of livestock, diseases and disabilities among other risks. Livestock Insurance covers against losses due to accidental death, diseases of terminal nature, emergency slaughter on the advice of a recognized veterinary surgeon, and theft of livestock. It also covers the death of an animal due to lightning, flood, rainstorm, windstorm, hailstorm, snow, hurricane, earthquake, landslides, diseases, inundation, surgical operation. and impact accidental damage by animals, trees or vehicles, aircraft, or motorized machinery. It covers dairy cattle, beef cattle, pigs, sheep, goats, camel, donkeys, horses, rabbits etc. The cover can also be extended to cover fire and burglary of insured animals as well as their transit. The amount payable per head is determined by how the livestock are insured as follows;

- Individual: If you have higher valued animals, listing them individually could be the right option in order to cover up to a specific dollar amount. The insured animals are usually marked or identified using ear tags, microchip, ear notching, tattoo and or use of photographs. Animals with natural identification marks are clearly noted in the proposal and veterinary health certificate.
- Blanket/Comprehensive coverage: Under this option, all the farm property including livestock, equipment and structures is insured in one lump sum amount in one policy.
- Herds: Livestock can also be insured as a herd, for example 100 heads of Friesian cattle.

In case of an annual policy, the maximum age should not exceed the prescribed age limit and below are some of the accepted age groups for the various animals.

No.	Animal	Age group
1	Milch cows (indigenous/cross bred/ exotic)	Age at first calving or 2 to 10 yrs.
	Milch buffaloes	Age at first calving or 3 to 12 yrs.
	Stud Bulls (Cow/ Buffalo species)	Earliest age at sexual maturity or 3 to 8 yrs.
	Bullock (castrated bull & castrated male buffaloes)	3 to 12 yrs.
	Indigenous, cross bred & exotic female calves/heifers & stud bulls	From 4 months up to date of first calving or minimum age as in the first 2 items above.
2	Sheep & goat	4 months to 7 yrs.
3	Pig	1 month to 6 yrs.
4	Camel	3 to 12 yrs.
5	Horse/pony/mule/donkey/yak	2 to 10 yrs.
6	Elephant (Temple & commercial)	5 to 60 yrs.
7	Pet dogs & cats	2 months to 10 yrs.
8	Rabbit	4 months to 4 yrs.

Basis of the Sum insured

The sums insured are usually based on the market value of the insured animals or loan amount as agreed in the policy. The market value is usually based on the assessment of a qualified veterinary doctor. In case of a disease cover, the sum insured may further be distributed as per extent of loss. In case of loan applicants or farmers, the sum insured per animal will be the loan amount declared in the loan application form by the farmer for purposes of the maximum borrowing limit fixed for him by the lending bank plus any subsidiary provided under the government program or price fixed by the block level/ purchase committee/ cash disbursement blocks based on project/ unit cost. As for the non-loan farmers, the value of livestock varies from breed to breed, area and time. The sum insured per animal is usually on the basis of recommendations given by a veterinary doctor. Wherever possible, highly valued animals are usually inspected by the Insurer or bank representatives. During policy renewal, the sum insured is the current market value of the animal not the previous one.

Indemnity/value at risk

n case of an agreed policy value, the sum insured is equal to the value at risk and the claim is settled up to limit of the sum insured subject to the relevant policy provisions. The value at risk is derived by establishing the current market value of the animals prior to the illness and this compared with the sum insured after which the lesser value is taken as the indemnity value. In case of insured loans, the value at risk is the outstanding loan amount at the time of loss.

Example 73:

- Sum Insured/ limit as per declaration schedule/ loan amount= USD 100,000
- Claim amount = USD 100,000
- Outstanding balance at the time of loss/ Value at Risk = USD 80,000
- Assessed amount = 80,000 x percentage loss (Subject to the relevant policy provisions like excess etc.)

Example 74:

- Sum Insured/ limit as per declaration schedule = USD 100,000
- Claim amount = USD 125,000
- Market value at the time of loss/Value at Risk = USD 75,000
- Assessed amount = 75,000 (Subject to the relevant policy provisions like excess etc.)

10.3 Poultry insurance

Poultry refers to units of chicks/hens/cocks, ducks, turkeys, quails and such other domesticated birds reared for eggs and/or meat. It includes layer bird broilers hatchery birds (Breeding Stock). Exotic birds are usually those whose parents are of foreign breed either born in the country or abroad. Crossbred birds are those whose parents are of foreign breed. Poultry insurance is applicable to the above birds among others like fowls that are reared on intensive scale or confined environment. The minimum number of birds to qualify for this product may be in the range of 500 birds. The product protects the insured against losses due to mortality of birds caused by uncontrollable events including fire, lightning, Flood, cyclone/ storm/ tempest/ earthquake, strike, riot or act of terrorism and all diseases except diseases which are specifically excluded.

Sum Insured per bird

The market value of birds varies from breed to breed, from area to area and from time to time. A guideline valuation chart should be mapped out, approved and attached for fixing the maximum sum insured per bird and as the base of settling claims afterwards for the layers, broilers and or hatchery birds among other categories.

Indemnity/ Value at Risk

The policyholder is usually indemnified according to the table of indemnification (providing age wise valuation for the purpose of indemnity) subject to the relevant policy provisions like excess and salvage among others. The rate in the indemnification table or chart is multiplied with the market value of the bird at the time of loss. The payment is usually up to the sum insured or limit of indemnity as specified in the Schedule. In case of insured loans, the value at risk is the outstanding loan amount at the time of loss.

Example 75:

- Sum Insured/ limit as per declaration schedule/ loan amount= USD 80,000
- Claim amount = USD 30,000
- Outstanding balance at the time of loss/ Value at Risk = USD 18,000
- Assessed amount = 18,000 x percentage loss (Subject to the relevant policy provisions like excess etc.)

Example 76:

- Claim amount = USD 44,000 for death of 650 birds
- Sum insured based on average stock (50%) on stock for the last 12 months = USD 1,000,000. Maximum liability per claim is USD 100,000 and policy excess is 10% per location.
- During the assessment, it was noted that the death of the birds was at 23 weeks and the indemnification scale/chart indicated that these would fall in the bracket of (MP x 1.864). The market unit price of each price was noted to be USD 14.69 at the time of loss and this was multiplied with the chat rate of 1.864 i.e. 14.69 x 1.864 = USD 27.38 which is the cost per bird.
- The assessed number of death birds = 264 birds. The assessed loss = USD 27.38 x 264 birds = USD 7,229.15

10.4 Aquaculture insurance

Aquaculture is also commonly referred to as fish farming and is the farming of aquatic organisms, like fish, molluscs, crustaceans and aquatic plants. Mortality/ death of stock is a normal occurrence in aquaculture, and most farms at some stage suffer from losses beyond the natural mortality rate as a result of an unaccounted perils.

o The onshore policies usually cover mortality of insured items as a due to pollution, theft & malicious acts, predators, storm damage, subsidence, landslides, structural failure, breakage or blockage of any part of the water supply system, drought, fire, lightning, explosion, earthquake, freezing, frost damage, frazil ice, mechanical breakdown or accidental damage to machinery and other installations, electrical breakdown, failure or interruption of the electricity supply, electrocution, deoxygenation due to vegetation, microbiological activity or high water temperature, any other change in concentration of the normal chemical constituents of the water, including super saturation with dissolved gases and change in ph or salinity and insured disease.

o The offshore polices usually cover mortality of insured items as a result of pollution, theft and malicious acts, jellyfish, predation or physical damage by predators or other aquatic organisms (but not sea lice or other ecto parasites), storm, lightening, tidal wave (tsunami), collision, sudden and unforeseen structural failure of equipment, freezing, super cooling, ice damage, deoxygenation due to competing biological activity (bloom) or from changes in the physical or chemical conditions or the water, including upwelling and high water temperature, any other change in concentration of the normal chemical constituents of the water including change in ph or salinity and insured disease.

Basis of Sum insured

The projected highest sum insured usually forms the basis of the total sum insured under the policy. This is defined as the highest of the projected monthly total values for the whole farm during the period of insurance as stated in the rearing plan, and calculated in accordance with the basis of indemnity. This value is not less than the actual highest sum insured which is the highest total value of all monthly declarations during the period of insurance. The Insured is usually required to increase or decrease the amount of insurance in the event of any material changes of such values owing to fluctuations in the number and the value of the insured stock, provided always that such increase or decrease takes effect only after the same has been recorded in their policy by the Insurers.

Note:

- ✓ The monthly declaration are the actual stocks at the end of each month for each holding unit as summarized by the insured. These values are derived from the number of cultured species in a holding unit and the individual values according to the size or weight as stated in the basis of indemnity. The Insured is also expected to record the harvested amount, additional intake, natural mortality or the transfer of stock or part thereof to other holding units.
- ✓ The projected average sum insured is the average of the projected monthly total values for the whole farm as stated in the rearing plan, and calculated in accordance with the basis of indemnity.
- ✓ the actual average sum insured is usually computed from the total value in the monthly declarations during the period of insurance.

Indemnity/Value at Risk

The Value at Risk at the time of loss is equal to the monthly total value at the location as per the last monthly declaration minus the natural mortality incurred during the period between the loss and the last morthly stock declaration. In the event of loss or death of the stock or part thereof the basis of settlement is the value of stock at the time of loss. If the value of the insured stock at the time of loss is greater than the sum insured, the policyholder is only entitled to recover such proportion of the said loss as the sum insured bears to the total value of the said stock. In the event of the amount of the last completed monthly declaration prior to a loss being found to be less than the amount that ought to have been declared, the indemnity is reduced in the same proportion that the amount of the said declaration bears to the amount that ought to have been declared. In case of insured loans, the value at risk is the outstanding loan amount at the time of loss.

Example 77:

- Sum Insured = USD 120,000
- Value at Risk at the time of loss = USD 165,000
- Claim amount = USD 90,000
- Assessed amount = USD 72,000
- Average clause = (sum nsured/value at risk) x assessed amount
- = (120,000/150,000) x 72,000
- After average = USD 52,364 (subject to the relevant policy provisions like excess etc.)

Example 78:

- Sum Insured/ limit as per last monthly declaration schedule= USD 120,000
- Actual declaration or value for last month = USD 240,000
- Claim amount = USD 105.000
- Assessed amount = USD 94,000
- Average clause = (sum insured/value at risk) x assessed amount
- = (120,000/240,000) x 94,000
- After average = USD 47,000 (subject to the relevant policy provisions like excess etc.)

Example 79:

- Sum Insured/ loan amount= USD 120,000
- Claim amount = JSD 90,000

- Outstanding balance at the time of loss/ Value at Risk = USD 80,000
- Assessed amount = 80,000 x percentage loss (Subject to the relevant policy provisions like excess etc.)

11.0 SALVAGE & SCRAP VALUATION

11.1 Salvage valuation

The term is salvage can be defined as the act of saving something from an accident or bad situation in which other things have already been damaged, destroyed or lost. This aims to ensure that the affected items are not completely discarded and they retain some value in monetary terms.

In accounts, salvage value can also be defined as the monetary value for an asset at the end of its useful life after accounting for its depreciation and is determined by factors like the asset's age, condition, obsolescence, wear and tear, and market demand. It is sometimes referred to as the disposal value or residual value of an asset.

11.1.1 Ideal salvage value

This approach is commonly used by accountants and it greatly depends on the purchase price of the asset, depreciation per year and its useful life. It is computed using the formula below;

Salvage value = Purchase price – (Depreciation per year x Useful life)

Procedure for attaining the ideal salvage value.

- Acquire the purchase invoice of the asset. This usually includes it purchase costs including the FOB price, CIF costs up to a certain destination.
- The relevant storage charges, taxes, inland transportation charges and installation costs and or expert labour charges which are added to form the value of the asset on the balance sheet or asset register.
- These supplier's catalog usually contains the equipment useful life and is sometimes attained through comparison with the useful life's of known similar products.
- The depreciation of the asset can be attained from its declining output per year which may be attributed to its rate of use and wear & tear among other factor which result into a reduction in cash inflow.

Example 80:

A factory machine cost is USD 145,000 and it has a useful life of 15 years and lifespan of 30 years. The amount of depreciation per year is USD 5,000 per year. Calculate the Salvage value of the machine after 15 years.

Salvage value = Purchase price – (Depreciation per year x Useful life)

$$= 145,000 - (5,000 \times 15)$$
$$= 145,000 - 75,000$$
$$= USD\ 70,000$$

Note:

✓ It is important to differentiate the term useful life and lifespan as these have different definitions. The asset useful life is the period were the asset performs as expected with minimum breakdowns. The lifespan is the total life expectancy of an asset beyond which it may cease to be functional. After the useful life, the asset retains a residual value.

✓ The challenge in the above example comes when attaining the annual depreciation amount. This may not be in terms of income lost as a result of the declining machine performance and may not give the general picture of the machine salvage.

✓ The insured/ client may face challenges disposing off the salvage since a number of other factors had not been considered during the valuation and these include the physical defects on the asset, extent of damage, and prevailing market conditions among others.

11.1.2 Actual salvage value

This approach provides a more practical approach after a covered peril /accident and this considers a number of factors including the following;

- Extent of damage/loss,
- Asset reparability,
- Depreciation factors i.e. Age, period in use, frequency of use, environment of use, lifespan, obsolescence, wear & tear etc.
- Physical state/ condition after the loss,
- Asset uniqueness, specifications,
- Spare parts availability,
- Market size & demand at the time of valuation/loss etc.

Procedure for attaining the actual salvage value.

- The market value of the asset is attained through comparison with assets having approximately similar specifications to the existing asset. This also helps in ascertaining whether the asset technology is still available on the market after a given time frame. The market value of the asset with more similar specs is taken as the current replacement/market value of the new asset.
- The relevant depreciation method is applied to account for the period in use and the above-named factors. During the loss assessment, the extent of loss or damage is assessed and this examines the asset components that are partially and completely damaged. The repairable and non-repairable parts are identified.
- The physical defects present on the asset are considered together with the possibility of repairing them together with the other repairable components. The cost of replacing the non-repairable assets is also attained through market inquiries for the spare parts on the local or foreign market including the relevant costs involved in procuring them. All these are attained and deducted from the market value.
- Checks for salability of the items and estimated number of potential buyers or market size is also considered.
- The salvage value of the affected greatly depends on the extent of damage by a given peril or hazard.

Example 81:

A factory machine cost is USD 145,000 and it has a useful life of 15 years and lifespan of 30 years. The amount of depreciation per year is USD 5,000 per year. Calculate the Salvage value of the machine after 15 years after a fire incident.

No.	Item	Value (USD)
1	Market value of new machine	145,000
2	Less total depreciation for period in use	75,000
3	Less value of damaged parts/required spares	30,000
4	Less value of physical defects/repair cost including labour	10,000
5	Less collection, storage & marketing costs etc.	8,000
	Net salvage/disposal value	**22,000**

11.2 Scrap Valuation

The term scrap means materials or objects that are no longer used for the purpose they were made for, but can be used in another way. The scrap value can also be defined as the value of a physical asset's individual parts or components when it's no longer usable or damaged beyond repair. This value is derived when the owner of an asset decides on whether to repair the damaged asset or to break it down and sell each of its parts independently.

11.2.1 Ideal scrap value

This approach usually depends on the invoice cost of the asset, depreciation per year and its useful life and is computed using the formula below;

Scrap value = Cost of the asset – (Depreciation per year x Useful life)

Example 82:

A factory purchases machine worth USD 175,000 and estimates that the useful life of the machine is 8 years at a depreciable rate of 15%. Find its scrap value after 8 years.

- Dep per year   = 15% x USD 175,000 = USD 26,250
- Scrap value   = Cost of the asset – (Depreciation per year x Useful life)
- Scrap value   = 175,000 - (26,250 x 8) = USD 43,750

11.2.2 Actual scrap value

This approach mainly considers the market prices of the damaged and non-damaged items. The completely damaged parts are sold in terms of their weight and these may be purchased by smelting companies. The none damaged parts are sold are spare parts at fair market prices. Below are some of the factors considered under this approach;

- Extent of damage/loss.
- Number of damaged and undamaged parts
- Weight of the partially and completely damaged parts
- Value of completely damaged parts
- Value of asset components that are in good condition.
- Market size & demand at the time of valuation/loss etc.

Example 83:

Following a severe truck accident, the owner of a truck is told that the truck needs a new cabin, engine and front bonnet components. The truck was purchased at USD 12,000 and it repair cost is USD 8,700. Since this cost is about 72.5% of the cost value, the truck qualifies to be treated as a total loss or assumed to have retained a scrap value. These completely affected parts can be sold to various scrap dealers at 0.3 USD per kg. The other parts that are not completely damaged include the gearbox, some parts of the suspension system, tyres and these could be sold as independent spares. The scrap valuation may be computed as follows;

When completely regarded as scrap;

- Vehicle cost   USD 12,000
- Vehicle weight   5,000 Kg
- Metal scrap value cost per Kg   0.3 USD/Kg as per prevailing
  market conditions
- <u>Total scrap value</u>   :   <u>USD 1,500 (independent of cost)</u>

When considering the extent of loss/ damaged individual components;

- Vehicle weight   :   5,000 Kg
- Actual weight of completely damaged items   :   1,555 Kg
- Metal scrap value cost per Kg   :   0.3 USD/Kg

No.	Description		Value (USD)
	Completely damaged parts		
1	Vehicle weight	5000 kgs	
2	Actual weight of completely damaged items	1,555 Kg	
3	Metal scrap value cost per Kg	0.3 USD/Kg	
	Subtotal		466.5
	Non-damaged parts		
4	Market value of suspension assy including the gear box	USD 600	
5	Market value of chassis assy	USD 250	
6	Market value of trunk/rear cage	USD 250	
7	Market value of the 4 tyres	USD 200	
	Subtotal		1,300
	Total scrap value		**1,746.5**

<u>**Note:**</u>

- ✓ There should be proper assessment of the extent of damage of the affected item to attain the completely damaged, partially damaged and non-damaged parts in order to attain their actual salvage or scrap values.
- ✓ The market inquiries of these affected parts should be carried out from number of potential buyers in order to gain a proper value of each category of affected parts.
- ✓ The non-salvageable parts which may neither have a scrap or disposal value are usually discarded into the various waste collection areas. These may include burnt clothes, burnt furniture etc.
- ✓ The nature of the salvage or scrap value greatly depends on the acting peril, extent of loss and immediate loss mitigation measures. For example, severe fire incidents usually cause severe non-recoverable damages to a number of assets including office equipment, furniture, fixtures & fittings, machinery and may sometimes cause extensive damages to the buildings.

12.0 GENERAL SUMMARY

12.1 Valuation key points.

❖ Valuation can be defined as a professional judgement of the worthiness of something.

❖ The accuracy of a valuation depends, on the valuation method used, and level of details gathered in terms of asset specifications and quality of market research or historical documents containing similar properties values before and application of an appropriate depreciation method.

❖ Some of the most commonly used valuation methods include comparison approach, book value approach, cost approach. Some of the most commonly applied depreciation methods include the straight-line and reducing or declining balance method. The valuer is free to apply other methods or approaches depending on the available information and nature of the assignment.

❖ Valuation methods can be selected basing on nature of assignment, nature of property or assets, availed documents or information, complexity of the assignment, prevailing market condition i.e. supply & demand and time among other factors.

❖ A good Loss Assessor, Valuer or Loss Adjuster should be able to estimate the value at risk of a given item using the available information that is provided by the insured as well as the salvage or scrap value.

12.2 Rating of valuation methods and their accuracy.

The table below shows some of the various approximate estimating technics by Skitmore and Patchell (1990: 78,79)

No.	Estimating technique	Application	General accuracy	Deterministic/ probabilistic
1	Cost method	AI	10% - 20%	Deterministic
2	Unit method	AI	25% - 30%	Deterministic
3	Comparison methods	AI	25% - 30%	Deterministic
4.	BOQ pricing (conventional)	Construction	10% - 20%	Deterministic
5.	Approximate quantities	Construction	15% - 25%	Deterministic
6.	Floor area method	Buildings	20% - 30%	Deterministic
7.	Cube method	Buildings	20% - 30%	Deterministic
8.	Interpolation	Buildings	25% - 30%	Deterministic

13.0 REFERENCES

1. http://www.ibc.ca/on/insurance-101/insurance-basics/how-premiums-are-calculated
2. https://www.cgu.com.au/learn-about-insurance/how-premiums-are-calculated
3. https://www.accountingtools.com/articles/business-valuation-methods.html
4. https://www.investopedia.com/terms/b/bookvalue.asp
   https://www.investopedia.com/articles/investing/110613/market-value-versus-book-value.asp.
5. https://corporatefinanceinstitute.com/resources/knowledge/valuation/cost-approach-real-estate/
6. Quantity surveyor's pocket book by Duncan Cartildge
7. M. M. Jinnah, *op. cit.*, p.94.
8. Sidney Davidson, *op. cit.*, p. 18-11, 30. *Ibid.*
9. M. M. Jinnah, *op. cit.*, p. 89, Sidney Davidson, 0J9. ciY., p. 18-13.
10. Guide to valuation and depreciation by David Edgerton FCPA
11. L. S. Porwal, *op.cit.*, p.253.
12. https://taxguru.in/chartered-accountant/goods-transit-transit-inventory.html
13. https://mjdbrokers.com/knowledge-base/goods-in-transit-basis-of-valuation/
14. https://www.yginsurance.com/index.php/en/cash-insurance
15. https://linkkinsurancebroker.com/fidelity-guarantee-insurance-policy/
16. GBU Burglary_Eng Fact Sheet. Tokio Marine Insurance Group
17. https://www.thehartford.com/workers-compensation/how-to-calculate-cost.
    https://www.policybazaar.com/commercial-insurance/workmen-compensation-policy/.https://joemillerinjurylaw.com/valuing-a-workers-compensation-case-settlement-how-life-expectancy-and-present-value-are-determined/
18. By Gregory Boop, About.com Guide
19. https://blog.constructaquote.com/ultimate-guide-public-liability-insurance/.
    https://www.hiscox.co.uk/business-insurance/public-liability-insurance/faq/what-is-public-liability-insurance
20. https://www.markeluk.com/business-insurance/professional-indemnity-insurance/what-is-professional-indemnity-insurance
21. https://www.cii.co.uk/learning/knowledge-services/reference-resources/classes-of-insurance/business-interruption/, The basic business interruption book, by Damian Glynn with Sue Taylor and Steven Nock
22. https://www.wallstreetmojo.com/sum-of-year-digits-method-depreciation/
23. https://www.wallstreetmojo.com/double-declining-balance-method/
24. https://owlcation.com/stem/Depreciation-Methods-in-Engineering-Economics-Formulas-Problems-and-Solutions
25. https://tutorstips.com/kilometre-method-of-depreciation/.
26. https://www.lynalden.com/discounted-cash-flow-analysis/
27. Guidance note of valuation of plant and machinery
28. https://www.lynalden.com/discounted-cash-flow-analysis/
29. https://www.accountingtools.com/articles/business-valuation-methods.html.
    https://www.investopedia.com/terms/b/business-valuation.asp
30. Insurance-Claims-for-Loss-of-Stock-and-Loss-of-Profit

31. https://estimationqs.com/unit-method-of-estimating-advantages-and-disadvantages-construction/
32. https://civiconcepts.com/blog/types-of-estimate
33. Cost estimating by Dr. Emad Elbeltagi
34. Cost control in building design by the University of Moratuwa Sri lanka
35. Estimating-the-Reinstatement-Or-Replacement-Cost-in-Valuation by European Centre for Research Training and Development UK
36. https://www.emerald.com/insight/content/doi/10.1108/f.2001.06919eab.005/full/html
37. Development of the Cost Baseline for Achieving Excellence in Rural Transit Facilities by Sharareh Kermanshachi, Elnaz Safapour, Stuart Anderson, Keith Molenaar, and Cliff Schexnayder.
38. Building cost planning for the design team by Jim Smith. David Jaggar, Peter Love
39. Common system of agriculture insurance by Mr. Margalef Masia. Insurance of Crops in Developing Countries by R.A.J Roberts, https://www.iii.org/article/understanding-crop-insurance. https://www.iii.org/article/background-on-crop-insurance. https://aic.ug/our-services/multi-peril-crop-insurance. https://ag.purdue.edu/commercialag/home/resource/2017/06/crop-insurance-product-comparisons/. https://www.extension.iastate.edu/agdm/crops/html/a1-54.html. https://www.agmarkllc.com/cimultiperil. https://basis.ucdavis.edu/agricultural-index-insurance-economic-development. Providing index based agricultural insurance to smallholders: Recent progress and future promise, Marshall Burke, Alain de Janvry, and Juan Quintero1, CEGA, University of California at Berkeley

www.ingramcontent.com/pod-product-compliance
Lightning Source LLC
Chambersburg PA
CBHW070610220526

45467CB00003B/1368